Tales from the Alhambra

Washington Irving

FOR MORE INFORMATION

For further information about Alhambra and Granada
visit www.alhambra-guide.com

Rough draughts of some of the following tales and essays were actually written during a residence in the Alhambra; others were subsequently added, founded on notes and observations made there. Care was taken to maintain local coloring and verisimilitude; so that the whole might present a faithful and living picture of that microcosm, that singular little world into which I had been fortuitously thrown; and about which the external world had a very imperfect idea. It was my endeavor scrupulously to depict its half Spanish, half Oriental character; its mixture of the heroic, the poetic, and the grotesque; to revive the traces of grace and beauty fast fading from its walls; to record the regal and chivalrous traditions concerning those who once trod its courts; and the whimsical and superstitious legends of the motley race now burrowing among its ruins.

The papers thus roughly sketched out lay for three or four years in my portfolio, until I found myself in London, in 1832, on the eve of returning to the United States. I then endeavored to arrange them for the press, but the preparations for departure did not allow sufficient leisure. Several were thrown aside as incomplete; the rest were put together somewhat hastily and in rather a crude and chaotic manner.

In the present edition I have revised and re-arranged the whole work, enlarged some parts, and added others, including the papers originally omitted; and have thus endeavored to render it more complete and more worthy of the indulgent reception with which it has been favored.

W.I
1851

Recollections of The Alhambra

During a summer's residence in the old Moorish palace of the Alhambra, of which I have already given numerous anecdotes to the public, I used to pass much of my time in the beautiful hall of the Abencerrages, beside the fountain celebrated in the tragic story of that devoted race. Here it was, that thirty-six cavaliers of that heroic line were treacherously sacrificed, to appease the jealousy or allay the fears of a tyrant. The fountain which now throws up its sparkling jet, and sheds a dewy freshness around, ran red with the noblest blood of Granada, and a deep stain on the marble pavement is still pointed out, by the cicerones of the pile, as a sanguinary record of the massacre. I have regarded it with the same determined faith with which I have regarded the traditional stains of Rizzio's blood on the floor of the chamber of the unfortunate Mary, at Holyrood. I thank no one for endeavoring to enlighten my credulity, on such points of popular belief. It is like breaking up the shrine of the pilgrim; it is robbing a poor traveller of half the reward of his toils; for, strip travelling of its historical illusions, and what a mere fag you make of it!

For my part, I gave myself up, during my sojourn in the Alhambra, to all the romantic and fabulous traditions connected with the pile. I lived in the midst of an Arabian tale, and shut my eyes, as much as possible, to every thing that called me back to every-day life; and if there is any country in Europe where one can do so, it is in poor, wild, legendary, proud-spirited, romantic Spain; where the old magnificent barbaric spirit still contends against the utilitarianism of modern civilization.

In the silent and deserted halls of the Alhambra; surrounded with the insignia of regal sway, and the still vivid, though dilapidated traces of oriental voluptuousness, I was in the strong-hold of Moorish story, and every thing spoke and breathed of the glorious days of Granada, when under the dominion of the crescent. When I sat in the hall of the Abencerrages, I suffered my mind to conjure up all that I had read of that illustrious line. In the proudest days of Moslem domination, the Abencerrages were the soul of every thing noble and chivalrous. The veterans of the family, who sat in the royal council, were the foremost to devise those heroic enterprises, which carried dismay into the territories of the Christians; and what the sages of the family devised, the young men of the name were the foremost to execute. In all services of hazard; in all adventurous forays, and hair-breadth hazards; the Abencerrages were sure to win the brightest laurels. In those noble recreations, too, which bear so close an affinity to war; in the tilt and tourney, the riding at the ring, and the daring bull-fight; still the Abencerrages carried off the palm. None could equal them for the splendor of their array, the gallantry of their devices; for their noble bearing, and glorious horsemanship. Their open-handed munificence made them the idols of the populace, while their lofty magnanimity, and perfect faith, gained them golden opinions from the generous and high-minded. Never were they known to decry the merits of a rival, or to betray the confidings of a friend; and the "word of an Abencerrage" was a guarantee that never admitted of a doubt.

And then their devotion to the fair! Never did Moorish beauty consider the fame of her charms established, until she had an Abencerrage for a lover; and never did an Abencerrage prove recreant to his vows. Lovely Granada! City of delights! Who ever bore the favors of thy dames more proudly on their casques, or championed them more gallantly in the chivalrous tilts of the Vivarambla? Or who ever made thy moon-lit balconies, thy gardens of myrtles and roses, of oranges, citrons, and pomegranates, respond to more tender serenades?

I speak with enthusiasm on this theme; for it is connected with the recollection of one of the sweetest evenings and sweetest scenes that ever I enjoyed in Spain. One of the greatest pleasures of the Spaniards is, to sit in the beautiful summer evenings, and listen to traditional ballads, and tales about the wars of the Moors and Christians, and the "*buenas andanzas*" and "*grandes hechos*," the "good fortunes" and "great exploits" of the hardy warriors of yore. It is worthy of remark, also, that many of these songs, or romances, as they are called, celebrate the prowess and magnanimity in war, and the tenderness and, fidelity in love, of the Moorish cavaliers, once their most formidable and hated foes. But centuries have elapsed, to extinguish the bigotry of the zealot; and the once detested warriors of Granada are now held up by Spanish poets, as the mirrors of chivalric virtue.

Such was the amusement of the evening in question. A number of us were seated in the Hall of the Abencerrages, listening to one of the most gifted and fascinating beings that I had ever met with in my wanderings. She was young and beautiful; and light and ethereal; full of fire, and spirit, and pure enthusiasm. She wore the fanciful Andalusian dress; touched the guitar with speaking eloquence; improvised with wonderful facility; and, as she became excited by her theme, or by the rapt attention of her auditors, would pour forth, in the richest and most melodious strains, a succession of couplets, full of striking description, or stirring narration, and composed, as I was assured, at the moment. Most of these were suggested by the place, and related to the ancient glories of Granada, and the prowess of her chivalry. The Abencerrages were her favorite heroes; she felt a woman's admiration of their gallant courtesy, and high-souled honor; and it was touching and inspiring to hear the praises of that generous but devoted race, chanted in this fated hall of their calamity, by the lips of Spanish beauty.

Among the subjects of which she treated, was a tale of Moslem honor, and old-fashioned Spanish courtesy, which made a strong impression on me. She disclaimed all merit of invention, however, and said she had merely dilated into verse a popular tradition; and, indeed, I have since found the main facts inserted at the end of Conde's History of the Domination of the Arabs, and the story itself embodied in the form of an episode in the Diana of Montemayor. From these sources I have drawn it forth, and endeavored to shape it according to my recollection of the version of the beautiful minstrel; but, alas! what can supply the want of that voice, that look, that form, that action, which gave magical effect to her chant, and held every one rapt in breathless admiration! Should this mere *travestie* of her inspired numbers ever meet her eye, in her stately abode at Granada, may it meet with that indulgence which belongs to her benignant nature. Happy

7

should I be, if it could awaken in her bosom one kind recollection of the lonely stranger and sojourner, for whose gratification she did not think it beneath her to exert those fascinating powers which were the delight of brilliant circles; and who will ever recall with enthusiasm the happy evening passed in listening to her strains, in the moon-lit halls of the Alhambra.

The Journey

In the spring of 1829, the author of this work, whom curiosity had brought into Spain, made a rambling expedition from Seville to Granada in company with a friend, a member of the Russian Embassy at Madrid. Accident had thrown us together from distant regions of the globe, and a similarity of taste led us to wander together among the romantic mountains of Andalusia. Should these pages meet his eye, wherever thrown by the duties of his station, whether mingling in the pageantry of courts, or meditating on the truer glories of nature, may they recall the scenes of our adventurous companionship, and with them the recollection of one, in whom neither time nor distance will obliterate the remembrance of his gentleness and worth.

And here, before setting forth, let me indulge in a few previous remarks on Spanish scenery and Spanish travelling. Many are apt to picture Spain to their imaginations as a soft southern region, decked out with the luxuriant charms of voluptuous Italy. On the contrary, though there are exceptions in some of the maritime provinces, yet, for the greater part, it is a stern, melancholy country, with rugged mountains, and long sweeping plains, destitute of trees, and indescribably silent and lonesome, partaking of the savage and solitary character of Africa. What adds to this silence and loneliness, is the absence of singing birds, a natural consequence of the want of groves and hedges. The vulture and the eagle are seen wheeling about the mountain-cliffs, and soaring over the plains, and groups of shy bustards stalk about the heaths; but the myriads of smaller birds, which animate the whole face of other countries, are met with in but few provinces in Spain, and in those chiefly among the orchards and gardens which surround the habitations of man.

In the interior provinces the traveller occasionally traverses great tracts cultivated with grain as far as the eye can reach, waving at times with verdure, at other times naked and sunburnt, but he looks round in vain for the hand that has tilled the soil. At length, he perceives some village on a steep hill, or rugged crag, with mouldering battlements and ruined watchtower; a strong-hold, in old times, against civil war, or Moorish inroad; for the custom among the peasantry of congregating together for mutual protection is still kept up in most parts of Spain, in consequence of the maraudings of roving freebooters.

But though a great part of Spain is deficient in the garniture of groves and forests, and the softer charms of ornamental cultivation, yet its scenery is noble in its severity, and in unison with the attributes of its people; and I think that I better understand the proud, hardy, frugal and abstemious Spaniard, his manly defiance of hardships, and contempt of effeminate indulgences, since I have seen the country he inhabits.

There is something too, in the sternly simple features of the Spanish landscape, that impresses on the soul a feeling of sublimity. The immense plains of the Castiles and of La Mancha, extending as far as the eye can reach, derive an interest from their very nakedness and immensity, and possess, in some degree, the solemn grandeur of the ocean. In ranging over these boundless wastes, the eye catches sight here and there of a straggling herd of cattle attended by a lonely herdsman, motionless as a statue, with his long slender pike tapering up like a lance into the air; or, beholds a long train of mules slowly moving along the waste like a train of camels in the desert; or, a single horseman, armed with blunderbuss and stiletto, and prowling over the plain. Thus the country, the habits, the very looks of the people, have something of the Arabian character. The general insecurity of the country is evinced in the universal use of weapons. The herdsman in the field, the shepherd in the plain, has his musket and his knife. The wealthy villager rarely ventures to the market-town without his trabuco, and, perhaps, a servant on foot with a blunderbuss on his shoulder; and the most petty journey is undertaken with the preparation of a warlike enterprise.

The dangers of the road produce also a mode of travelling, resembling, on a diminutive scale, the caravans of the east. The arrieros, or carriers, congregate in convoys, and set off in large and well-armed trains on appointed days; while additional travellers swell their number, and contribute to their strength. In this primitive way is the commerce of the country carried on. The muleteer is the general medium of traffic, and the legitimate traverser of the land, crossing the peninsula from the Pyrenees and the Asturias to the Alpuxarras, the Serrania de Ronda, and even to the gates of Gibraltar. He lives frugally and hardily: his alforjas of coarse cloth hold his scanty stock of provisions; a leathern bottle, hanging at his saddle-bow, contains wine or water, for a supply across barren mountains and thirsty plains; a mule-cloth spread upon the ground is his bed at night, and his pack-saddle his pillow. His low, but clean-limbed and sinewy form betokens strength; his complexion is dark and sunburnt; his eye resolute, but quiet in its expression, except when kindled by sudden emotion; his demeanor is frank, manly, and courteous, and he never passes you without a grave salutation: "Dios guarde a usted!" "Va usted con Dios, Caballero!" ("God guard you!" "God be with you, Cavalier!")

As these men have often their whole fortune at stake upon the burden of their mules, they have their weapons at hand, slung to their saddles, and ready to be snatched out for desperate defence; but their united numbers render them secure against petty bands of marauders, and the solitary bandolero, armed to the teeth, and mounted on his Andalusian steed, hovers about them, like a pirate about a merchant convoy, without daring to assault.

The Spanish muleteer has an inexhaustible stock of songs and ballads, with which to beguile his incessant wayfaring. The airs are rude and simple, consisting of but few inflections. These he chants forth with a loud voice, and long, drawling cadence, seated sideways on his mule, who seems to listen with infinite gravity, and to keep time, with his paces, to the tune. The couplets thus chanted, are often old traditional romances about the Moors, or some legend of a saint, or some love-ditty; or, what is still more frequent, some ballad about a bold contrabandista, or hardy bandolero, for the smuggler and the robber are poetical heroes among the common people of Spain. Often, the song of the muleteer is composed at the instant, and relates to some local scene, or some incident of the journey. This talent of singing and improvising is frequent in Spain, and is said to have been inherited from the Moors. There is something wildly pleasing in listening to these ditties among the rude and lonely scenes they illustrate; accompanied, as they are, by the occasional jingle of the mule-bell.

It has a most picturesque effect also to meet a train of muleteers in some mountain-pass. First you hear the bells of the leading mules, breaking with their simple melody the stillness of the airy height; or, perhaps, the voice of the muleteer admonishing some tardy or wandering animal, or chanting, at the full stretch of his lungs, some traditionary ballad. At length you see the mules slowly winding along the cragged defile, sometimes descending precipitous cliffs, so as to present themselves in full relief against the sky, sometimes toiling up the deep arid chasms below you. As they approach, you descry their gay decorations of worsted stuffs, tassels, and saddle-cloths, while, as they pass by, the ever-ready trabuco, slung behind the packs and saddles, gives a hint of the insecurity of the road.

The ancient kingdom of Granada, into which we* were about to penetrate, is one of the most mountainous regions of Spain. Vast sierras, or chains of mountains, destitute of shrub or tree, and mottled with variegated marbles and granites, elevate their sunburnt summits against a deep-blue sky; yet in their rugged bosoms lie ingulfed verdant and fertile valleys, where the desert and the garden strive for mastery, and the very rock is, as it were, compelled to yield the fig, the orange, and the citron, and to blossom with the myrtle and the rose.

Note to the Revised Edition. — The Author feels at liberty to mention that his travelling companion was the Prince Dolgorouki, at present Russian minister at the Court of Persia.

In the wild passes of these mountains the sight of walled towns and villages, built like eagles' nests among the cliffs, and surrounded by Moorish battlements, or of ruined watchtowers perched on lofty peaks, carries the mind back to the chivalric days of Christian and Moslem warfare, and to the romantic struggle for the conquest of Granada. In traversing these lofty sierras the traveller is often obliged to alight, and lead his horse up and down the steep and jagged ascents and descents, resembling the broken steps of a staircase.

Sometimes the road winds along dizzy precipices, without parapet to guard him from the gulfs below, and then will plunge down steep, and dark, and dangerous declivities. Sometimes it struggles through rugged barrancos, or ravines, worn by winter torrents, the obscure path of the contrabandista; while, ever and anon, the ominous cross, the monument of robbery and murder, erected on a mound of stones at some lonely part of the road, admonishes the traveller that he is among the haunts of banditti, perhaps at that very moment under the eye of some lurking bandolero. Sometimes, in winding through the narrow valleys, he is startled by a hoarse bellowing, and beholds above him on some green fold of the mountain a herd of fierce Andalusian bulls, destined for the combat of the arena. I have felt, if I may so express it, an agreeable horror in thus contemplating, near at hand, these terrific animals, clothed with tremendous strength, and ranging their native pastures in untamed wildness, strangers almost to the face of man: they know no one but the solitary herdsman who attends upon them, and even he at times dares not venture to approach them. The low bellowing of these bulls, and their menacing aspect as they look down from their rocky height, give additional wildness to the savage scenery.

I have been betrayed unconsciously into a longer disquisition than I intended on the general features of Spanish travelling; but there is a romance about all the recollections of the Peninsula dear to the imagination.

As our proposed route to Granada lay through mountainous regions, where the roads are little better than mule paths, and said to be frequently beset by robbers, we took due travelling precautions. Forwarding the most valuable part of our luggage a day or two in advance by the arrieros, we retained merely clothing and necessaries for the journey and money for the expenses of the road, with a little surplus of hard dollars by way of robber purse, to satisfy the gentlemen of the road should we be assailed. Unlucky is the too wary traveller who, having grudged this precaution, falls into their clutches empty handed: they are apt to give him a sound ribroasting for cheating them out of their dues. "Caballeros like them cannot afford to scour the roads and risk the gallows for nothing."

A couple of stout steeds were provided for our own mounting, and a third for our scanty luggage and the conveyance of a sturdy Biscayan lad, about twenty years of age, who was to be our guide, our groom, our valet, and at all times our guard. For the latter office he was provided with a formidable trabuco or carbine, with which he promised to defend us against rateros or solitary footpads; but as to powerful bands, like that of the "sons of Ecija," he confessed they were quite beyond his prowess. He made much vainglorious boast about his weapon at the outset of the journey, though, to the discredit of his generalship, it was suffered to hang unloaded behind his saddle.

According to our stipulations, the man from whom we hired the horses was to be at the expense of their feed and stabling on the journey, as well as of the maintenance of our Biscayan squire, who of course was provided with funds for the purpose; we took care, however, to give the latter a private hint, that, though we made a close bargain with his master, it was all in his favor, as, if he proved a good man and true, both he and the horses should live at our cost, and the money provided for their maintenance remain in his pocket. This unexpected largess, with the occasional present of a cigar, won his heart completely. He was, in truth, a faithful, cheery, kind-hearted creature, as full of saws and proverbs as that miracle of squires, the renowned Sancho himself, whose name, by the by, we bestowed upon him, and like a true Spaniard, though treated by us with companionable familiarity, he never for a moment, in his utmost hilarity, overstepped the bounds of respectful decorum.

Such were our minor preparations for the journey, but above all we laid in an ample stock of good humor, and a genuine disposition to be pleased, determining to travel in true contrabandista style, taking things as we found them, rough or smooth, and mingling with all classes and conditions in a kind of vagabond companionship. It is the true way to travel in Spain. With such disposition and determination, what a country is it for a traveller, where the most miserable inn is as full of adventure as an enchanted castle, and every meal is in itself an achievement! Let others repine at the lack of turnpike roads and sumptuous hotels, and all the elaborate comforts of a country cultivated and civilized into tameness and commonplace; but give me the rude mountain scramble; the roving, haphazard, wayfaring; the half wild, yet frank and hospitable manners, which impart such a true game flavor to dear old romantic Spain!

Thus equipped and attended, we cantered out of "Fair Seville city" at half-past six in the morning of a bright May day, in company with a lady and gentleman of our acquaintance, who rode a few miles with us, in the Spanish mode of taking leave. Our route lay through old Alcala de Guadaira (Alcala on the river Aira), the benefactress of Seville, that supplies it with bread and water. Here live the bakers who furnish Seville with that delicious bread for which it is renowned; here are fabricated those roscas well known by the well-merited appellation of pan de Dios (bread of God), with which, by the way, we ordered our man, Sancho, to stock his alforjas for the journey. Well has this beneficent little city been denominated the "Oven of Seville"; well has it been called Alcala de los Panaderos (Alcala of the bakers), for a great part of its inhabitants are of that handicraft, and the highway hence to Seville is constantly traversed by lines of mules and donkeys laden with great panniers of loaves and roscas.

I have said Alcala supplies Seville with water. Here are great tanks or reservoirs, of Roman and Moorish construction, whence water is conveyed to Seville by noble aqueducts. The springs of Alcala are almost as much vaunted as its ovens; and to the lightness, sweetness, and purity of its water is attributed in some measure the delicacy of its bread.

Here we halted for a time, at the ruins of the old Moorish castle, a favorite resort for picnic parties from Seville, where we had passed many a pleasant hour. The walls are of great extent, pierced with loopholes; inclosing a huge square tower or keep, with the remains of masmoras, or subterranean granaries. The Guadaira winds its stream round the hill, at the foot of these ruins, whimpering among reeds, rushes, and pond-lilies, and overhung with rhododendron, eglantine, yellow myrtle, and a profusion of wild flowers and aromatic shrubs; while along its banks are groves of oranges, citrons, and pomegranates, among which we heard the early note of the nightingale.

A picturesque bridge was thrown across the little river, at one end of which was the ancient Moorish mill of the castle, defended by a tower of yellow stone; a fisherman's net hung against the wall to dry, and hard by in the river was his boat; a group of peasant women in bright-colored dresses, crossing the arched bridge, were reflected in the placid stream. Altogether it was an admirable scene for a landscape painter.

The old Moorish mills, so often found on secluded streams, are characteristic objects in Spanish landscape, and suggestive of the perilous times of old. They are of stone, and often in the form of towers with loopholes and battlements, capable of defence in those warlike days when the country on both sides of the border was subject to sudden inroad and hasty ravage, and when men had to labor with their weapons at hand, and some place of temporary refuge.

Our next halting place was at Gandul, where were the remains of another Moorish castle, with its ruined tower, a nestling place for storks, and commanding a view over a vast campina or fertile plain, with the mountains of Ronda in the distance. These castles were strong-holds to protect the plains from the talas or forays to which they were subject, when the fields of corn would be laid waste, the flocks and herds swept from the vast pastures, and, together with captive peasantry, hurried off in long cavalgadas across the borders.

At Gandul we found a tolerable posada; the good folks could not tell us what time of day it was — the clock only struck once in the day, two hours after noon; until that time it was guesswork. We guessed it was full time to eat; so, alighting, we ordered a repast. While that was in preparation we visited the palace once the residence of the Marquis of Gandul. All was gone to decay; there were but two or three rooms habitable, and very poorly furnished. Yet here were the remains of grandeur: a terrace, where fair dames and gentle cavaliers may once have walked; a fish-pond and ruined garden, with grape-vines and date-bearing palm-trees. Here we were joined by a fat curate, who gathered a bouquet of roses and presented it, very gallantly, to the lady who accompanied us.

Below the palace was the mill, with orange-trees and aloes in front, and a pretty stream of pure water. We took a seat in the shade, and the millers, all leaving their work, sat down and smoked with us; for the Andalusians are always ready for a gossip. They were waiting for the regular visit of the barber, who came once a week to put all their chins in order. He arrived shortly afterwards: a lad of seventeen, mounted on a donkey, eager to display his new alforjas or saddle-bags, just bought at a fair; price one dollar, to be paid on St. John's day (in June), by which time he trusted to have mown beards enough to put him in funds.

By the time the laconic clock of the castle had struck two we had finished our dinner. So, taking leave of our Seville friends, and leaving the millers still under the hands of the barber, we set off on our ride across the campina. It was one of those vast plains, common in Spain, where for miles and miles there is neither house nor tree. Unlucky the traveller who has to traverse it, exposed as we were to heavy and repeated showers of rain. There is no escape nor shelter. Our only protection was our Spanish cloaks, which nearly covered man and horse, but grew heavier every mile. By the time we had lived through one shower we would see another slowly but inevitably approaching; fortunately in the interval there would be an outbreak of bright, warm, Andalusian sunshine, which would make our cloaks send up wreaths of steam, but which partially dried them before the next drenching.

Shortly after sunset we arrived at Arahal, a little town among the hills. We found it in a bustle with a party of miquelets, who were patrolling the country to ferret out robbers. The appearance of foreigners like ourselves was an unusual circumstance in an interior country town; and little Spanish towns of the kind are easily put in a state of gossip and wonderment by such an occurrence. Mine host, with two or three old wiseacre comrades in brown Cloaks, studied our passports in a corner of the posada, while an Alguazil took notes by the dim light of a lamp. The passports were in foreign languages and perplexed them, but our Squire Sancho assisted them in their studies, and magnified our importance with the grandiloquence of a Spaniard. In the mean time the magnificent distribution of a few cigars had won the hearts of all around us; in a little while the whole community seemed put in agitation to make us welcome. The corregidor himself waited upon us, and a great rush-bottomed arm-chair was ostentatiously bolstered into our room by our landlady, for the accommodation of that important personage. The commander of the patrol took supper with us — a lively, talking, laughing Andaluz, who had made a campaign in South America, and recounted his exploits in love and war with much pomp of phrase, vehemence of gesticulation, and mysterious rolling of the eye. He told us that he had a list of all the robbers in the country, and meant to ferret out every mother's son of them; he offered us at the same time some of his soldiers as an escort. "One is enough to protect you, senores; the robbers know me, and know my men; the sight of one is enough to spread terror through a whole sierra." We thanked him for his offer, but assured him, in his own strain, that with the protection of our redoubtable squire, Sancho, we were not afraid of all the ladrones of Andalusia.

While we were supping with our Drawcansir friend, we heard the notes of a guitar, and the click of castanets, and presently a chorus of voices singing a popular air. In fact mine host had gathered together the amateur singers and musicians, and the rustic belles of the neighborhood, and, on going forth, the courtyard or patio of the inn presented a scene of true Spanish festivity. We took our seats with mine host and hostess and the commander of the patrol, under an archway opening into the court; the guitar passed from hand to hand, but a jovial shoemaker was the Orpheus of the place. He was a pleasant-looking fellow, with huge black whiskers; his sleeves were rolled up to his elbows. He touched the guitar with masterly skill, and sang a little amorous ditty with an expressive leer at the women, with whom he was evidently a favorite. He afterwards danced a fandango with a buxom Andalusian damsel, to the great delight of the spectators. But none of the females present could compare with mine host's pretty daughter, Pepita, who had slipped away and made her toilette for the occasion, and had covered her head with roses; and who distinguished herself in a bolero with a handsome young dragoon. We ordered our host to let wine and refreshment circulate freely among the company, yet, though there was a motley assembly of soldiers, muleteers, and villagers, no one exceeded the bounds of sober enjoyment. The scene was a study for a painter: the picturesque group of dancers, the troopers in their half military dresses, the peasantry wrapped in their brown cloaks; nor must I omit to mention the old meagre Alguazil, in a short black cloak, who took no notice of any thing going on, but sat in a corner diligently writing by the dim light of a huge copper lamp, that might have figured in the days of Don Quixote.

The following morning was bright and balmy, as a May morning ought to be, according to the poets. Leaving Arahal at seven o'clock, with all the posada at the door to cheer us off we pursued our way through a fertile country, covered with grain and beautifully verdant; but which in summer, when the harvest is over and the fields parched and brown, must be monotonous and lonely; for, as in our ride of yesterday, there were neither houses nor people to be seen. The latter all congregate in villages and strong-holds among the hills, as if these fertile plains were still subject to the ravages of the Moor.

At noon we came to where there was a group of trees, beside a brook in a rich meadow. Here we alighted to make our midday meal. It was really a luxurious spot, among wild flowers and aromatic herbs, with birds singing around us. Knowing the scanty larders of Spanish inns, and the houseless tracts we might have to traverse, we had taken care to have the alforjas of our squire well stocked with cold provisions, and his bota, or leathern bottle, which might hold a gallon, filled to the neck with choice Valdepenas wine.* As we depended more upon these for our well-being than even his trabuco, we exhorted him to be more attentive in keeping them well charged; and I must do him the justice to say that his namesake, the trencher-loving Sancho Panza, was never a more provident purveyor. Though the alforjas and the bota were frequently and vigorously assailed throughout the journey, they had a wonderful power of repletion, our vigilant squire sacking every thing that remained from our repasts at the inns, to supply these junketings by the road-side, which were his delight.

* It may be as well to note here, that the alforjas are square pockets at each end of a long cloth about a foot and a half wide, formed by turning up its extremities. The cloth is then thrown over the saddle, and the pockets hang on each side like saddle-bags. It is an Arab invention. The bota is a leathern bag or bottle, of portly dimensions, with a narrow neck. It is also oriental. Hence the scriptural caution, which perplexed me in my boyhood, not to put new wine into old bottles.

On the present occasion he spread quite a sumptuous variety of remnants on the green-sward before us, graced with an excellent ham brought from Seville; then, taking his seat at a little distance, he solaced himself with what remained in the alforjas. A visit or two to the bota made him as merry and chirruping as a grasshopper filled with dew. On my comparing his contents of the alforjas to Sancho's skimming of the flesh-pots at the wedding of Camacho, I found he was well versed in the history of Don Quixote, but, like many of the common people of Spain, firmly believed it to be a true history.

"All that happened a long time ago, senor," said he, with an inquiring look.

"A very long time," I replied.

"I dare say more than a thousand years"— still looking dubiously.

"I dare say not less."

The squire was satisfied. Nothing pleased the simple-hearted varlet more than my comparing him to the renowned Sancho for devotion to the trencher, and he called himself by no other name throughout the journey.

Our repast being finished, we spread our cloaks on the green-sward under the tree, and took a luxurious siesta in the Spanish fashion. The clouding up of the weather, however, warned us to depart, and a harsh wind sprang up from the southeast. Towards five o'clock we arrived at Osuna, a town of fifteen thousand inhabitants, situated on the side of a hill, with a church and a ruined castle. The posada was outside of the walls; it had a cheerless look. The evening being cold, the inhabitants were crowded round a brasero in a chimney corner; and the hostess was a dry old woman, who looked like a mummy. Every one eyed us askance as we entered, as Spaniards are apt to regard strangers; a cheery, respectful salutation on our part, caballeroing them and touching our sombreros, set Spanish pride at ease; and when we took our seat among them, lit our cigars, and passed the cigar-box round among them, our victory was complete. I have never known a Spaniard, whatever his rank or condition, who would suffer himself to be outdone in courtesy; and to the common Spaniard the present of a cigar (puro) is irresistible. Care, however, must be taken never to offer him a present with an air of superiority and condescension; he is too much of a caballero to receive favors at the cost of his dignity.

Leaving Osuna at an early hour the next morning, we entered the sierra or range of mountains. The road wound through picturesque scenery, but lonely; and a cross here and there by the road side, the sign of a murder, showed that we were now coming among the "robber haunts." This wild and intricate country, with its silent plains and valleys intersected by mountains, has ever been famous for banditti. It was here that Omar Ibn Hassan, a robber-chief among the Moslems, held ruthless sway in the ninth century, disputing dominion even with the caliphs of Cordova. This too was a part of the regions so often ravaged during the reign of Ferdinand and Isabella by Ali Atar, the old Moorish alcayde of Loxa, father-in-law of Boabdil, so that it was called Ali Atar's garden, and here "Jose Maria," famous in Spanish brigand story, had his favorite lurking places.

In the course of the day we passed through Fuente la Piedra near a little salt lake of the same name, a beautiful sheet of water, reflecting like a mirror the distant mountains. We now came in sight of Antiquera, that old city of warlike reputation, lying in the lap of the great sierra which runs through Andalusia. A noble vega spread out before it, a picture of mild fertility set in a frame of rocky mountains. Crossing a gentle river we approached the city between hedges and gardens, in which nightingales were pouring forth their evening song. About nightfall we arrived at the gates. Every thing in this venerable city has a decidedly Spanish stamp. It lies too much out of the frequented track of foreign travel to have its old usages trampled out. Here I observed old men still wearing the montero, or ancient hunting cap, once common throughout Spain; while the young men wore the little round-crowned hat, with brim turned up all round, like a cup turned down in its saucer, while the brim was set off with little black tufts like cockades. The women, too, were all in mantillas and basquinas. The fashions of Paris had not reached Antiquera.

Pursuing our course through a spacious street, we put up at the posada of San Fernando. As Antiquera, though a considerable city, is, as I observed, somewhat out of the track of travel, I had anticipated bad quarters and poor fare at the inn. I was agreeably disappointed, therefore, by a supper table amply supplied, and what were still more acceptable, good clean rooms and comfortable beds. Our man, Sancho, felt himself as well off as his namesake, when he had the run of the duke's kitchen, and let me know, as I retired for the night, that it had been a proud time for the alforjas.

Early in the morning (May 4th) I strolled to the ruins of the old Moorish castle, which itself had been reared on the ruins of a Roman fortress. Here, taking my seat on the remains of a crumbling tower, I enjoyed a grand and varied landscape, beautiful in itself, and full of storied and romantic associations; for I was now in the very heart of the country famous for the chivalrous contests between Moor and Christian. Below me, in its lap of hills, lay the old warrior city so often mentioned in chronicle and ballad. Out of yon gate and down yon hill paraded the band of Spanish cavaliers, of highest rank and bravest bearing, to make that foray during the war and conquest of Granada, which ended in the lamentable massacre among the mountains of Malaga, and laid all Andalusia in mourning. Beyond spread out the vega, covered with gardens and orchards and fields of grain and enamelled meadows, inferior only to the famous vega of Granada. To the right the Rock of the Lovers stretched like a cragged promontory into the plain, whence the daughter of the Moorish alcayde and her lover, when closely pursued, threw themselves in despair.

The matin peal from church and convent below me rang sweetly in the morning air, as I descended. The market-place was beginning to throng with the populace, who traffic in the abundant produce of the vega; for this is the mart of an agricultural region. In the market-place were abundance of freshly plucked roses for sale; for not a dame or damsel of Andalusia thinks her gala dress complete without a rose shining like a gem among her raven tresses.

On returning to the inn I found our man Sancho, in high gossip with the landlord and two or three of his hangers-on. He had just been telling some marvellous story about Seville, which mine host seemed piqued to match with one equally marvellous about Antiquera. There was once a fountain, he said, in one of the public squares called IL fuente del toro, the fountain of the bull, because the water gushed from the mouth of a bull's head, carved of stone. Underneath the head was inscribed:

EN FRENTE DEL TORO
SE HALLEN TESORO.

(In front of the bull there is treasure.)

Many digged in front of the fountain, but lost their labor and found no money. At last one knowing fellow construed the motto a different way. It is in the forehead (frente) of the bull that the treasure is to be found, said he to himself, and I am the man to find it. Accordingly he came late at night, with a mallet, and knocked the head to pieces; and what do you think he found?

"Plenty of gold and diamonds!" cried Sancho eagerly.

"He found nothing," rejoined mine host dryly; "and he ruined the fountain."

Here a great laugh was set up by the landlord's hangers-on; who considered Sancho completely taken in by what I presume was one of mine host's standing jokes.

Leaving Antiquera at eight O'clock, we had a delightful ride along the little river, and by gardens and orchards, fragrant with the odors of spring and vocal with the nightingale. Our road passed round the Rock of the Lovers (el Penon de los Enamorados), which rose in a precipice above us. In the course of the morning we passed through Archidona, situated in the breast of a high hill, with a three-pointed mountain towering above it, and the ruins of a Moorish fortress. It was a great toil to ascend a steep stony street leading up into the city, although it bore the encouraging name of Calle Real del Llano (the Royal Street of the Plain), but it was still a greater toil to descend from this mountain city on the other side.

At noon we halted in sight of Archidona, in a pleasant little meadow among hills covered with olive-trees. Our cloaks were spread on the grass, under an elm by the side of a bubbling rivulet; our horses were tethered where they might crop the herbage, and Sancho was told to produce his alforjas. He had been unusually silent this morning ever since the laugh raised at his expense, but now his countenance brightened, and he produced his alforjas with an air of triumph. They contained the contributions of four days' journeying, but had been signally enriched by the foraging of the previous evening in the plenteous inn at Antiquera; and this seemed to furnish him with a set-off to the banter of mine host.

EN FRENTE DEL TORO
SE HALLEN TESORO

would he exclaim, with a chuckling laugh, as he drew forth the heterogeneous contents one by one, in a series which seemed to have no end. First came forth a shoulder of roasted kid, very little the worse for wear; then an entire partridge; then a great morsel of salted codfish wrapped in paper; then the residue of a ham; then the half of a pullet, together with several rolls of bread, and a rabble rout of oranges, figs, raisins, and walnuts. His bota also had been recruited with some excellent wine of Malaga. At every fresh apparition from his larder, he would enjoy our ludicrous surprise, throwing himself back on the grass, shouting with laughter, and exclaiming "Frente del toro! — frente del toro! Ah, senores, they thought Sancho a simpleton at Antiquera; but Sancho knew where to find the tesoro."

While we were diverting ourselves with his simple drollery, a solitary beggar approached, who had almost the look of a pilgrim. He had a venerable gray beard, and was evidently very old, supporting himself on a staff, yet age had not bowed him down; he was tall and erect, and had the wreck of a fine form. He wore a round Andalusian hat, a sheep-skin jacket, and leathern breeches, gaiters, and sandals. His dress, though old and patched, was decent, his demeanor manly, and he addressed us with the grave courtesy that is to be remarked in the lowest Spaniard. We were in a favorable mood for such a visitor; and in a freak of capricious charity gave him some silver, a loaf of fine wheaten bread, and a goblet of our choice wine of Malaga. He received them thankfully, but without any grovelling tribute of gratitude. Tasting the wine, he held it up to the light, with a slight beam of surprise in his eye, then quaffing it off at a draught, "It is many years," said he, "since I have tasted such wine. It is a cordial to an old man's heart." Then, looking at the beautiful wheaten loaf, "Bendito sea tal pan!" "Blessed be such bread!" So saying, he put it in his wallet. We urged him to eat it on the spot. "No, senores," replied he, "the wine I had either to drink or leave; but the bread I may take home to share with my family."

Our man Sancho sought our eye, and reading permission there, gave the old man some of the ample fragments of our repast, on condition, however, that he should sit down and make a meal.

He accordingly took his seat at some little distance from us, and began to eat slowly, and with a sobriety and decorum that would have become a hidalgo. There was altogether a measured manner and a quiet self-possession about the old man, that made me think that he had seen better days; his language too, though simple, had occasionally something picturesque and almost poetical in the phraseology. I set him down for some broken-down cavalier. I was mistaken; it was nothing but the innate courtesy of a Spaniard, and the poetical turn of thought and language often to be found in the lowest classes of this clear-witted people. For fifty years, he told us, he had been a shepherd, but now he was out of employ and destitute. "When I was a young man," said he, "nothing could harm or trouble me; I was always well, always gay; but now I am seventy-nine years of age, and a beggar, and my heart begins to fail me."

Still he was not a regular mendicant: it was not until recently that want had driven him to this degradation; and he gave a touching picture of the struggle between hunger and pride, when abject destitution first came upon him. He was returning from Malaga without money; he had not tasted food for some time, and was crossing one of the great plains of Spain, where there were but few habitations. When almost dead with hunger, he applied at the door of a venta or country inn. "Perdon usted por Dios, hermano!" ('Excuse us, brother, for God's sake!') was the reply — the usual mode in Spain of refusing a beggar.

"I turned away," said he, "with shame greater than my hunger, for my heart was yet too proud. I came to a river with high banks, and deep, rapid current, and felt tempted to throw myself in: 'What should such an old, worthless, wretched man as I live for?' But when I was on the brink of the current, I thought on the blessed Virgin, and turned away. I travelled on until I saw a country-seat at a little distance from the road, and entered the outer gate of the court-yard. The door was shut, but there were two young senoras at a window. I approached and begged. 'Perdon usted por Dios, hermano!'— and the window closed.

"I crept out of the court-yard, but hunger overcame me, and my heart gave way: I thought my hour at hand, so I laid myself down at the gate, commended myself to the Holy Virgin, and covered my head to die. In a little while afterwards the master of the house came home. Seeing me lying at his gate, he uncovered my head, had pity on my gray hairs, took me into his house, and gave me food. So, senores, you see that one should always put confidence in the protection of the Virgin."

The old man was on his way to his native place, Archidona, which was in full view on its steep and rugged mountain. He pointed to the ruins of its castle. "That castle," he said, "was inhabited by a Moorish king at the time of the wars of Granada. Queen Isabella invaded it with a great army; but the king looked down from his castle among the clouds, and laughed her to scorn! Upon this the Virgin appeared to the queen, and guided her and her army up a mysterious path in the mountains, which had never before been known. When the Moor saw her coming, he was astonished, and springing with his horse from a precipice, was dashed to pieces! The marks of his horse's hoofs," said the old man, "are to be seen in the margin of the rock to this day. And see, senores, yonder is the road by which the queen and her army mounted: you see it like a ribbon up the mountain's side; but the miracle is, that, though it can be seen at a distance, when you come near it disappears!"

The ideal road to which he pointed was undoubtedly a sandy ravine of the mountain, which looked narrow and defined at a distance, but became broad and indistinct on an approach.

As the old man's heart warmed with wine and wassail, he went on to tell us a story of the buried treasure left under the castle by the Moorish king. His own house was next to the foundations of the castle. The curate and notary dreamed three times of the treasure, and went to work at the place pointed out in their dreams. His own son-in-law heard the sound of their pickaxes and spades at night. What they found nobody knows; they became suddenly rich, but kept their own secret. Thus the old man had once been next door to fortune, but was doomed never to get under the same roof.

I have remarked that the stories of treasure buried by the Moors, so popular throughout Spain, are most current among the poorest people. Kind nature consoles with shadows for the lack of substantials. The thirsty man dreams of fountains and running streams, the hungry man of banquets, and the poor man of heaps of hidden gold: nothing certainly is more opulent than the imagination of a beggar.

Our afternoon's ride took us through a steep and rugged defile of the mountains, called Puerto del Rey, the Pass of the King; being one of the great passes into the territories of Granada, and the one by which King Ferdinand conducted his army. Towards sunset the road, winding round a hill, brought us in sight of the famous little frontier city of Loxa, which repulsed Ferdinand from its walls. Its Arabic name implies "guardian," and such it was to the vega of Granada, being one of its advanced guards. It was the strong-hold of that fiery veteran, old Ali Atar, father-in-law of Boabdil; and here it was that the latter collected his troops, and sallied forth on that disastrous foray which ended in the death of the old alcayde and his own captivity. From its commanding position at the gate, as it were, of this mountain pass, Loxa has not unaptly been termed the key of Granada. It is wildly picturesque; built along the face of an arid mountain. The ruins of a Moorish alcazar or citadel crown a rocky mound which rises out of the centre of the town. The river Xenil washes its base, winding among rocks, and groves, and gardens, and meadows, and crossed by a Moorish bridge. Above the city all is savage and sterile, below is the richest vegetation and the freshest verdure. A similar contrast is presented by the river; above the bridge it is placid and grassy, reflecting groves and gardens; below it is rapid, noisy and tumultuous. The Sierra Nevada, the royal mountains of Granada, crowned with perpetual snow, form the distant boundary to this varied landscape; one of the most characteristic of romantic Spain.

Alighting at the entrance of the city, we gave our horses to Sancho to lead them to the inn, while we strolled about to enjoy the singular beauty of the environs. As we crossed the bridge to a fine alameda, or public walk, the bells tolled the hour of oration. At the sound the wayfarers, whether on business or pleasure, paused, took off their hats, crossed themselves, and repeated their evening prayer — a pious custom still rigidly observed in retired parts of Spain. Altogether it was a solemn and beautiful evening scene, and we wandered on as the evening gradually closed, and the new moon began to glitter between the high elms of the alameda.

We were roused from this quiet state of enjoyment by the voice of our trusty squire hailing us from a distance. He came up to us, out of breath. "Ah, senores," cried he, "el pobre Sancho no es nada sin Don Quixote." ("Ah, senores, poor Sancho is nothing without Don Quixote.") He had been alarmed at our not coming to the inn; Loxa was such a wild mountain place, full of contrabandistas, enchanters, and infiernos; he did not well know what might have happened, and set out to seek us, inquiring after us of every person he met, until he traced us across the bridge, and, to his great joy, caught sight of us strolling in the alameda.

The inn to which he conducted us was called the Corona, or Crown, and we found it quite in keeping with the character of the place, the inhabitants of which seem still to retain the bold, fiery spirit of the olden time. The hostess was a young and handsome Andalusian widow, whose trim basquina of black silk, fringed with bugles, set off the play of a graceful form and round pliant limbs. Her step was firm and elastic; her dark eye was full of fire, and the coquetry of her air, and varied ornaments of her person, showed that she was accustomed to be admired.

She was well matched by a brother, nearly about her own age; they were perfect models of the Andalusian majo and maja. He was tall, vigorous, and well-formed, with a clear olive complexion, a dark beaming eye, and curling chestnut whiskers that met under his chin. He was gallantly dressed in a short green velvet jacket, fitted to his shape, profusely decorated with silver buttons, with a white handkerchief in each pocket. He had breeches of the same, with rows of buttons from the hips to the knees; a pink silk handkerchief round his neck, gathered through a ring, on the bosom of a neatly-plaited shirt; a sash round the waist to match; bottinas, or spatterdashes, of the finest russet leather, elegantly worked, and open at the calf to show his stockings and russet shoes, setting off a well-shaped foot.

As he was standing at the door, a horseman rode up and entered into low and earnest conversation with him. He was dressed in a similar style, and almost with equal finery — a man about thirty, square-built, with strong Roman features, handsome, though slightly pitted with the small-pox; with a free, bold, and somewhat daring air. His powerful black horse was decorated with tassels and fanciful trappings, and a couple of broad-mouthed blunderbusses hung behind the saddle. He had the air of one of those contrabandistas I have seen in the mountains of Ronda, and evidently had a good understanding with the brother of mine hostess; nay, if I mistake not, he was a favored admirer of the widow. In fact, the whole inn and its inmates had something of a contrabandista aspect, and a blunderbuss stood in a corner beside the guitar. The horseman I have mentioned passed his evening in the posada, and sang several bold mountain romances with great spirit. As we were at supper, two poor Asturians put in in distress, begging food and a night's lodging. They had been waylaid by robbers as they came from a fair among the mountains, robbed of a horse, which carried all their stock in trade, stripped of their money, and most of their apparel, beaten for having offered resistance, and left almost naked in the road. My companion, with a prompt generosity natural to him, ordered them a supper and a bed, and gave them a sum of money to help them forward towards their home.

As the evening advanced, the dramatis personae thickened. A large man, about sixty years of age, of powerful frame, came strolling in, to gossip with mine hostess. He was dressed in the ordinary Andalusian costume, but had a huge sabre tucked under his arm, wore large moustaches, and had something of a lofty swaggering air. Every one seemed to regard him with great deference.

Our man Sancho whispered to us that he was Don Ventura Rodriguez, the hero and champion of Loxa, famous for his prowess and the strength of his arm. In the time of the French invasion he surprised six troopers who were asleep: he first secured their horses, then attacked them with his sabre, killed some, and took the rest prisoners. For this exploit the king allows him a peseta (the fifth of a duro, or dollar) per day, and has dignified him with the title of Don.

I was amused to behold his swelling language and demeanor. He was evidently a thorough Andalusian, boastful as brave. His sabre was always in his hand or under his arm. He carries it always about with him as a child does her doll, calls it his Santa Teresa, and says, "When I draw it, the earth trembles" ("'tiembla la tierra").

I sat until a late hour listening to the varied themes of this motley group, who mingled together with the unreserve of a Spanish posada. We had contrabandista songs, stories of robbers, guerilla exploits, and Moorish legends. The last were from our handsome landlady, who gave a poetical account of the infiernos, or infernal regions of Loxa, dark caverns, in which subterranean streams and waterfalls make a mysterious sound. The common people say that there are money-coiners shut up there from the time of the Moors, and that the Moorish kings kept their treasures in those caverns.

I retired to bed with my imagination excited by all that I had seen and heard in this old warrior city. Scarce had I fallen asleep when I was aroused by a horrid din and uproar, that might have confounded the hero of La Mancha himself whose experience of Spanish inns was a continual uproar. It seemed for a moment as if the Moors were once more breaking into the town, or the infiernos of which mine hostess talked had broken loose. I sallied forth half dressed to reconnoiter. It was nothing more nor less than a charivari to celebrate the nuptials of an old man with a buxom damsel. Wishing him joy of his bride and his serenade, I returned to my more quiet bed, and slept soundly until morning.

While dressing, I amused myself in reconnoitering the populace from my window. There were groups of fine-looking young men in the trim fanciful Andalusian costume, with brown cloaks, thrown about them in true Spanish style, which cannot be imitated, and little round majo hats stuck on with a peculiar knowing air. They had the same galliard look which I have remarked among the dandy mountaineers of Ronda. Indeed, all this part of Andalusia abounds with such game-looking characters. They loiter about the towns and villages, seem to have plenty of time and plenty of money: "horse to ride and weapon to wear." Great gossips; great smokers; apt at touching the guitar, singing couplets to their maja belles, and famous dancers of the bolero. Throughout all Spain the men, however poor, have a gentleman-like abundance of leisure, seeming to consider it the attribute of a true cavaliero never to be in a hurry; but the Andalusians are gay as well as leisurely, and have none of the squalid accompaniments of idleness. The adventurous contraband trade which prevails throughout these mountain regions, and along the maritime borders of Andalusia, is doubtless at the bottom of this galliard character.

In contrast to the costume of these groups was that of two long-legged Valencians conducting a donkey, laden with articles of merchandise, their musket slung crosswise over his back ready for action. They wore round jackets (jalecos), wide linen bragas or drawers scarce reaching to the knees and looking like kilts, red fajas or sashes swathed tightly round their waists, sandals of espartal or bass weed, colored kerchiefs round their heads somewhat in the style of turbans but leaving the top of the head uncovered; in short, their whole appearance having much of the traditional Moorish stamp.

On leaving Loxa we were joined by a cavalier, well mounted and well armed, and followed on foot by an escopetero or musketeer. He saluted us courteously, and soon let us into his quality. He was chief of the customs, or rather, I should suppose, chief of an armed company whose business it is to patrol the roads and look out for contrabandistas. The escopetero was one of his guards. In the course of our morning's ride I drew from him some particulars concerning the smugglers, who have risen to be a kind of mongrel chivalry in Spain. They come into Andalusia, he said, from various parts, but especially from La Mancha, sometimes to receive goods, to be smuggled on an appointed night across the line at the plaza or strand of Gibraltar, sometimes to meet a vessel, which is to hover on a given night off a certain part of the coast. They keep together and travel in the night. In the daytime they lie quiet in barrancos, gullies of the mountains or lonely farm-houses; where they are generally well received, as they make the family liberal presents of their smuggled wares. Indeed, much of the finery and trinkets worn by the wives and daughters of the mountain hamlets and farm-houses are presents from the gay and open-handed contrabandistas.

Arrived at the part of the coast where a vessel is to meet them, they look out at night from some rocky point or headland. If they descry a sail near the shore they make a concerted signal; sometimes it consists in suddenly displaying a lantern three times from beneath the folds of a cloak. If the signal is answered, they descend to the shore and prepare for quick work. The vessel runs close in; all her boats are busy landing the smuggled goods, made up into snug packages for transportation on horseback. These are hastily thrown on the beach, as hastily gathered up and packed on the horses, and then the contrabandistas clatter off to the mountains. They travel by the roughest, wildest, and most solitary roads, where it is almost fruitless to pursue them. The custom-house guards do not attempt it: they take a different course. When they hear of one of these bands returning full freighted through the mountains, they go out in force, sometimes twelve infantry and eight horsemen, and take their station where the mountain defile opens into the plain. The infantry, who lie in ambush some distance within the defile, suffer the band to pass, then rise and fire upon them. The contrabandistas dash forward, but are met in front by the horsemen. A wild skirmish ensues. The contrabandistas, if hard pressed, become desperate. Some dismount, use their horses as breast-works, and fire over their backs; others cut the cords, let the packs fall off to delay the enemy, and endeavor to escape with their steeds. Some get off in this way with the loss of their packages; some are taken, horses, packages, and all; others abandon every thing, and make their escape by scrambling up the mountains. "And then," cried Sancho, who had been listening with a greedy ear, "se hacen ladrones legitimos"— and then they become legitimate robbers.

I could not help laughing at Sancho's idea of a legitimate calling of the kind; but the chief of customs told me it was really the case that the smugglers, when thus reduced to extremity, thought they had a kind of right to take the road, and lay travellers under contribution, until they had collected funds enough to mount and equip themselves in contrabandista style.

Towards noon our wayfaring companion took leave of us and turned up a steep defile, followed by his escopetero; and shortly afterwards we emerged from the mountains, and entered upon the far famed Vega of Granada.

Our last mid-day's repast was taken under a grove of olive-trees on the border of a rivulet. We were in a classical neighborhood; for not far off were the groves and orchards of the Soto de Roma. This, according to fabulous tradition, was a retreat founded by Count Julian to console his daughter Florinda. It was a rural resort of the Moorish kings of Granada, and has in modern times been granted to the Duke of Wellington.

Our worthy squire made a half melancholy face as he drew forth, for the last time, the contents of his alforjas, lamenting that our expedition was drawing to a close, for, with such cavaliers, he said, he could travel to the world's end. Our repast, however, was a gay one; made under such delightful auspices. The day was without a cloud. The heat of the sun was tempered by cool breezes from the mountains. Before us extended the glorious Vega. In the distance was romantic Granada surmounted by the ruddy towers of the Alhambra, while far above it the snowy summits of the Sierra Nevada shone like silver.

Our repast finished, we spread our cloaks and took our last siesta al fresco, lulled by the humming of bees among the flowers and the notes of doves among the olive-trees. When the sultry hours were passed we resumed our journey. After a time we overtook a pursy little man, shaped not unlike a toad and mounted on a mule. He fell into conversation with Sancho, and finding we were strangers, undertook to guide us to a good posada. He was an escribano (notary), he said, and knew the city as thoroughly as his own pocket. "Ah Dios, senores! what a city you are going to see. Such streets! such squares! such palaces! and then the women — ah Santa Maria purisima — what women!" "But the posada you talk of," said I; "are you sure it is a good one?"

"Good! Santa Maria! the best in Granada. Salones grandes — camas de luxo — colchones de pluma (grand saloons — luxurious sleeping rooms — beds of down). Ah, senores, you will fare like King Chico in the Alhambra."

"And how will my horses fare?" cried Sancho.

"Like King Chico's horses. Chocolate con leche y bollos para almuerza" ("chocolate and milk with sugar cakes for breakfast"), giving the squire a knowing wink and a leer.

After such satisfactory accounts nothing more was to be desired on that head. So we rode quietly on, the squab little notary taking the lead, and turning to us every moment with some fresh exclamation about the grandeurs of Granada and the famous times we were to have at the posada.

Thus escorted, we passed between hedges of aloes and Indian figs, and through that wilderness of gardens with which the Vega is embroidered, and arrived about sunset at the gates of the city. Our officious little conductor conveyed us up one street and down another, until he rode into the courtyard of an inn where he appeared to be perfectly at home. Summoning the landlord by his Christian name, he committed us to his care as two caballeros de mucho valor, worthy of his best apartments and most sumptuous fare. We were instantly reminded of the patronizing stranger who introduced Gil Blas with such a flourish of trumpets to the host and hostess of the inn at Pennaflor, ordering trouts for his supper, and eating voraciously at his expense. "You know not what you possess," cried he to the innkeeper and his wife. "You have a treasure in your house. Behold in this young gentleman the eighth wonder of the world — nothing in this house is too good for Senor Gil Blas of Santillane, who deserves to be entertained like a prince."

Determined that the little notary should not eat trouts at our expense, like his prototype of Pennaflor, we forbore to ask him to supper; nor had we reason to reproach ourselves with ingratitude; for we found before morning the little varlet, who was no doubt a good friend of the landlord, had decoyed us into one of the shabbiest posadas in Granada.

Place of the Alhambra

To the traveller imbued with a feeling for the historical and poetical, so inseparably intertwined in the annals of romantic Spain, the Alhambra is as much an object of devotion as is the Caaba to all true Moslems. How many legends and traditions, true and fabulous; how many songs and ballads, Arabian and Spanish, of love and war and chivalry, are associated with this oriental pile! It was the royal abode of the Moorish kings, where, surrounded with the splendors and refinements of Asiatic luxury, they held dominion over what they vaunted as a terrestrial paradise, and made their last stand for empire in Spain. The royal palace forms but a part of a fortress, the walls of which, studded with towers, stretch irregularly round the whole crest of a hill, a spur of the Sierra Nevada or Snowy Mountains, and overlook the city; externally it is a rude congregation of towers and battlements, with no regularity of plan nor grace of architecture, and giving little promise of the grace and beauty which prevail within.

In the time of the Moors the fortress was capable of containing within its outward precincts an army of forty thousand men, and served occasionally as a strong-hold of the sovereigns against their rebellious subjects. After the kingdom had passed into the hands of the Christians, the Alhambra continued to be a royal demesne, and was occasionally inhabited by the Castilian monarchs. The emperor Charles V commenced a sumptuous palace within its walls, but was deterred from completing it by repeated shocks of earthquakes. The last royal residents were Philip V and his beautiful queen, Elizabetta of Parma, early in the eighteenth century. Great preparations were made for their reception. The palace and gardens were placed in a state of repair, and a new suite of apartments erected, and decorated by artists brought from Italy. The sojourn of the sovereigns was transient, and after their departure the palace once more became desolate. Still the place was maintained with some military state. The governor held it immediately from the crown, its jurisdiction extended down into the suburbs of the city, and was independent of the captain-general of Granada. A considerable garrison was kept up, the governor had his apartments in the front of the old Moorish palace, and never descended into Granada without some military parade. The fortress, in fact, was a little town of itself, having several streets of houses within its walls, together with a Franciscan convent and a parochial church.

The desertion of the court, however, was a fatal blow to the Alhambra. Its beautiful halls became desolate, and some of them fell to ruin; the gardens were destroyed, and the fountains ceased to play. By degrees the dwellings became filled with a loose and lawless population; contrabandistas, who availed themselves of its independent jurisdiction to carry on a wide and daring course of smuggling, and thieves and rogues of all sorts, who made this their place of refuge whence they might depredate upon Granada and its vicinity. The strong arm of government at length interfered; the whole community was thoroughly sifted; none were suffered to remain but such as were of honest character, and had legitimate right to a residence; the greater part of the houses were demolished and a mere hamlet left, with the parochial church and the Franciscan convent. During the recent troubles in Spain, when Granada was in the hands of the French, the Alhambra was garrisoned by their troops, and the palace was occasionally inhabited by the French commander. With that enlightened taste which has ever distinguished the French nation in their conquests, this monument of Moorish elegance and grandeur was rescued from the absolute ruin and desolation that were overwhelming it. The roofs were repaired, the saloons and galleries protected from the weather, the gardens cultivated, the watercourses restored, the fountains once more made to throw up their sparkling showers; and Spain may thank her invaders for having preserved to her the most beautiful and interesting of her historical monuments.

On the departure of the French they blew up several towers of the outer wall, and left the fortifications scarcely tenable. Since that time the military importance of the post is at an end. The garrison is a handful of invalid soldiers, whose principal duty is to guard some of the outer towers, which serve occasionally as a prison of state; and the governor, abandoning the lofty hill of the Alhambra, resides in the centre of Granada, for the more convenient dispatch of his official duties. I cannot conclude this brief notice of the state of the fortress without bearing testimony to the honorable exertions of its present commander, Don Francisco de Serna, who is tasking all the limited resources at his command to put the palace in a state of repair, and by his judicious precautions, has for some time arrested its too certain decay. Had his predecessors discharged the duties of their station with equal fidelity, the Alhambra might yet have remained in almost its pristine beauty: were government to second him with means equal to his zeal, this relic of it might still be preserved for many generations to adorn the land, and attract the curious and enlightened of every clime.

Our first object of course, on the morning after our arrival, was a visit to this time-honored edifice; it has been so often, however, and so minutely described by travellers, that I shall not undertake to give a comprehensive and elaborate account of it, but merely occasional sketches of parts with the incidents and associations connected with them.

Leaving our posada, and traversing the renowned square of the Vivarrambla, once the scene of Moorish jousts and tournaments, now a crowded market-place, we proceeded along the Zacatin, the main street of what, in the time of the Moors, was the Great Bazaar, and where small shops and narrow alleys still retain the oriental character. Crossing an open place in front of the palace of the captain-general, we ascended a confined and winding street, the name of which reminded us of the chivalric days of Granada. It is called the Calle or street of the Gomeres, from a Moorish family famous in chronicle and song. This street led up to the Puerta de las Granadas, a massive gateway of Grecian architecture, built by Charles V, forming the entrance to the domains of the Alhambra.

At the gate were two or three ragged superannuated soldiers, dozing on a stone bench, the successors of the Zegris and the Abencerrages; while a tall, meagre varlet, whose rusty-brown cloak was evidently intended to conceal the ragged state of his nether garments, was lounging in the sunshine and gossiping with an ancient sentinel on duty. He joined us as we entered the gate, and offered his services to show us the fortress.

I have a traveller's dislike to officious ciceroni, and did not altogether like the garb of the applicant.

"You are well acquainted with the place, I presume?"

"Ninguno mas; pues senor, soy hijo de la Alhambra."—("Nobody better; in fact, sir, I am a son of the Alhambra!")

The common Spaniards have certainly a most poetical way of expressing themselves. "A son of the Alhambra!"— the appellation caught me at once; the very tattered garb of my new acquaintance assumed a dignity in my eyes. It was emblematic of the fortunes of the place, and befitted the progeny of a ruin.

I put some farther questions to him, and found that his title was legitimate. His family had lived in the fortress from generation to generation ever since the time of the conquest. His name was Mateo Ximenes. "Then, perhaps," said I, "you may be a descendant from the great Cardinal Ximenes?"—"Dios sabe! God knows, senor! It may be so. We are the oldest family in the Alhambra — Cristianos viejos, old Christians, without any taint of Moor or Jew. I know we belong to some great family or other, but I forget whom. My father knows all about it: he has the coat-of-arms hanging up in his cottage, up in the fortress."— There is not any Spaniard, however poor, but has some claim to high pedigree. The first title of this ragged worthy, however, had completely captivated me, so I gladly accepted the services of the "son of the Alhambra."

We now found ourselves in a deep narrow ravine, filled with beautiful groves, with a steep avenue, and various footpaths winding through it, bordered with stone seats, and ornamented with fountains. To our left, we beheld the towers of the Alhambra beetling above us; to our right, on the opposite side of the ravine, we were equally dominated by rival towers on a rocky eminence. These, we were told, were the Torres Vermejos, or vermilion towers, so called from their ruddy hue. No one knows their origin. They are of a date much anterior to the Alhambra: some suppose them to have been built by the Romans; others, by some wandering colony of Phoenicians. Ascending the steep and shady avenue, we arrived at the foot of a huge square Moorish tower, forming a kind of barbican, through which passed the main entrance to the fortress. Within the barbican was another group of veteran invalids, one mounting guard at the portal, while the rest, wrapped in their tattered cloaks, slept on the stone benches. This portal is called the Gate of Justice, from the tribunal held within its porch during the Moslem domination, for the immediate trial of petty causes: a custom common to the oriental nations, and occasionally alluded to in the Sacred Scriptures. "Judge and officers shalt thou make thee in all thy gates, and they shall judge the people with just judgment."

The great vestibule, or porch of the gate, is formed by an immense Arabian arch, of the horseshoe form, which springs to half the height of the tower. On the keystone of this arch is engraven a gigantic hand. Within the vestibule, on the keystone of the portal, is sculptured, in like manner, a gigantic key. Those who pretend to some knowledge of Mohammedan symbols, affirm that the hand is the emblem of doctrine; the five fingers designating the five principal commandments of the creed of Islam, fasting, pilgrimage, alms-giving, ablution, and war against infidels. The key, say they, is the emblem of the faith or of power; the key of Daoud or David, transmitted to the prophet. "And the key of the house of David will I lay upon his shoulder; so he shall open and none shall shut, and he shall shut and none shall open." (Isaiah xxii. 22.) The key we are told was emblazoned on the standard of the Moslems in opposition to the Christian emblem of the cross, when they subdued Spain or Andalusia. It betokened the conquering power invested in the prophet. "He that hath the key of David, he that openeth and no man shutteth; and shutteth and no man openeth." (Rev. iii. 7.)

A different explanation of these emblems, however, was given by the legitimate son of the Alhambra, and one more in unison with the notions of the common people, who attach something of mystery and magic to every thing Moorish, and have all kind of superstitions connected with this old Moslem fortress. According to Mateo, it was a tradition handed down from the oldest inhabitants, and which he had from his father and grandfather, that the hand and key were magical devices on which the fate of the Alhambra depended. The Moorish king who built it was a great magician, or, as some believed, had sold himself to the devil, and had laid the whole fortress under a magic spell. By this means it had remained standing for several hundred years, in defiance of storms and earthquakes, while almost all other buildings of the Moors had fallen to ruin, and disappeared. This spell, the tradition went on to say, would last until the hand on the outer arch should reach down and grasp the key, when the whole pile would tumble to pieces, and all the treasures buried beneath it by the Moors would be revealed.

Notwithstanding this ominous prediction, we ventured to pass through the spell-bound gateway, feeling some little assurance against magic art in the protection of the Virgin, a statue of whom we observed above the portal.

After passing through the barbican, we ascended a narrow lane, winding between walls, and came on an open esplanade within the fortress, called the Plaza de los Algibes, or Place of the Cisterns, from great reservoirs which undermine it, cut in the living rock by the Moors to receive the water brought by conduits from the Darro, for the supply of the fortress. Here, also, is a well of immense depth, furnishing the purest and coldest of water; another monument of the delicate taste of the Moors, who were indefatigable in their exertions to obtain that element in its crystal purity.

In front of this esplanade is the splendid pile commenced by Charles V, and intended, it is said, to eclipse the residence of the Moorish kings. Much of the oriental edifice intended for the winter season was demolished to make way for this massive pile. The grand entrance was blocked up; so that the present entrance to the Moorish palace is through a simple and almost humble portal in a corner. With all the massive grandeur and architectural merit of the palace of Charles V, we regarded it as an arrogant intruder, and passing by it with a feeling almost of scorn, rang at the Moslem portal.

While waiting for admittance, our self-imposed cicerone, Mateo Ximenes, informed us that the royal palace was intrusted to the care of a worthy old maiden dame called Dona Antonia-Molina, but who, according to Spanish custom, went by the more neighborly appellation of Tia Antonia (Aunt Antonia), who maintained the Moorish halls and gardens in order and showed them to strangers. While we were talking, the door was opened by a plump little black-eyed Andalusian damsel, whom Mateo addressed as Dolores, but who from her bright looks and cheerful disposition evidently merited a merrier name. Mateo informed me in a whisper that she was the niece of Tia Antonia, and I found she was the good fairy who was to conduct us through the enchanted palace. Under her guidance we crossed the threshold, and were at once transported, as if by magic wand, into other times and an oriental realm, and were treading the scenes of Arabian story. Nothing could be in greater contrast than the unpromising exterior of the pile with the scene now before us.

We found ourselves in a vast patio or court one hundred and fifty feet in length, and upwards of eighty feet in breadth, paved with white marble, and decorated at each end with light Moorish peristyles, one of which supported an elegant gallery of fretted architecture. Along the mouldings of the cornices and on various parts of the walls were escutcheons and ciphers, and cufic and Arabic characters in high relief, repeating the pious mottoes of the Moslem monarchs, the builders of the Alhambra, or extolling their grandeur and munificence. Along the centre of the court extended an immense basin or tank (estanque) a hundred and twenty-four feet in length, twenty-seven in breadth, and five in depth, receiving its water from two marble vases. Hence it is called the Court of the Alberca (from al Beerkah, the Arabic for a pond or tank). Great numbers of gold-fish were to be seen gleaming through the waters of the basin, and it was bordered by hedges of roses.

Passing from the Court of the Alberca under a Moorish archway, we entered the renowned Court of Lions. No part of the edifice gives a more complete idea of its original beauty than this, for none has suffered so little from the ravages of time. In the centre stands the fountain famous in song and story. The alabaster basins still shed their diamond drops; the twelve lions which support them, and give the court its name, still cast forth crystal streams as in the days of Boabdil. The lions, however, are unworthy of their fame, being of miserable sculpture, the work probably of some Christian captive. The court is laid out in flower-beds, instead of its ancient and appropriate pavement of tiles or marble; the alteration, an instance of bad taste, was made by the French when in possession of Granada. Round the four sides of the court are light Arabian arcades of open filigree work supported by slender pillars of white marble, which it is supposed were originally gilded. The architecture, like that in most parts of the interior of the palace, is characterized by elegance, rather than grandeur, bespeaking a delicate and graceful taste, and a disposition to indolent enjoyment. When one looks upon the fairy traces of the peristyles, and the apparently fragile fretwork of the walls, it is difficult to believe that so much has survived the wear and tear of centuries, the shocks of earthquakes, the violence of war, and the quiet, though no less baneful, pilferings of the tasteful traveller; it is almost sufficient to excuse the popular tradition that the whole is protected by a magic charm.

On one side of the court a rich portal opens into the Hall of the Abencerrages; so called from the gallant cavaliers of that illustrious line who were here perfidiously massacred. There are some who doubt the whole story, but our humble cicerone Mateo pointed out the very wicket of the portal through which they were introduced one by one into the Court of Lions, and the white marble fountain in the centre of the hall beside which they were beheaded. He showed us also certain broad ruddy stains on the pavement, traces of their blood, which, according to popular belief, can never be effaced.

Finding we listened to him apparently with easy faith, he added, that there was often heard at night, in the Court of Lions, a low confused sound, resembling the murmuring of a multitude; and now and then a faint tinkling, like the distant clank of chains. These sounds were made by the spirits of the murdered Abencerrages, who nightly haunt the scene of their suffering and invoke the vengeance of Heaven on their destroyer.

The sounds in question had no doubt been produced, as I had afterwards an opportunity of ascertaining, by the bubbling currents and tinkling falls of water conducted under the pavement through pipes and channels to supply the fountains; but I was too considerate to intimate such an idea to the humble chronicler of the Alhambra.

Encouraged by my easy credulity, Mateo gave me the following as an undoubted fact, which he had from his grandfather:

There was once an invalid soldier, who had charge of the Alhambra to show it to strangers: as he was one evening, about twilight, passing through the Court of Lions, he heard footsteps on the Hall of the Abencerrages; supposing some strangers to be lingering there, he advanced to attend upon them, when to his astonishment he beheld four Moors richly dressed, with gilded cuirasses and cimeters, and poniards glittering with precious stones. They were walking to and fro, with solemn pace, but paused and beckoned to him. The old soldier, however, took to flight, and could never afterwards be prevailed upon to enter the Alhambra. Thus it is that men sometimes turn their backs upon fortune; for it is the firm opinion of Mateo, that the Moors intended to reveal the place where their treasures lay buried. A successor to the invalid soldier was more knowing; he came to the Alhambra poor; but at the end of a year went off to Malaga, bought houses, set up a carriage, and still lives there one of the richest as well as oldest men of the place; all which, Mateo sagely surmised, was in consequence of his finding out the golden secret of these phantom Moors.

I now perceived I had made an invaluable acquaintance in this son of the Alhambra, one who knew all the apocryphal history of the place, and firmly believed in it, and whose memory was stuffed with a kind of knowledge for which I have a lurking fancy, but which is too apt to be considered rubbish by less indulgent philosophers. I determined to cultivate the acquaintance of this learned Theban.

Immediately opposite the Hall of the Abencerrages a portal, richly adorned, leads into a hall of less tragical associations. It is light and lofty, exquisitely graceful in its architecture, paved with white marble, and bears the suggestive name of the Hall of the Two Sisters. Some destroy the romance of the name by attributing it to two enormous slabs of alabaster which lie side by side, and form a great part of the pavement; an opinion strongly supported by Mateo Ximenes. Others are disposed to give the name a more poetical significance, as the vague memorial of Moorish beauties who once graced this hall, which was evidently a part of the royal harem. This opinion I was happy to find entertained by our little bright-eyed guide,

Dolores, who pointed to a balcony over an inner porch, which gallery, she had been told, belonged to the women's apartment. "You see, senor," said she, "it is all grated and latticed, like the gallery in a convent chapel where the nuns hear mass; for the Moorish kings," added she, indignantly, "shut up their wives just like nuns."

The latticed "jalousies," in fact, still remain, whence the dark-eyed beauties of the harem might gaze unseen upon the zambras and other dances and entertainments of the hall below.

On each side of this hall are recesses or alcoves for ottomans and couches, on which the voluptuous lords of the Alhambra indulged in that dreamy repose so dear to the Orientalists. A cupola or lantern admits a tempered light from above and a free circulation of air; while on one side is heard the refreshing sound of waters from the fountain of the lions, and on the other side the soft plash from the basin in the garden of Lindaraxa.

It is impossible to contemplate this scene so perfectly Oriental without feeling the early associations of Arabian romance, and almost expecting to see the white arm of some mysterious princess beckoning from the gallery, or some dark eye sparkling through the lattice. The abode of beauty is here, as if it had been inhabited but yesterday; but where are the two sisters; where the Zoraydas and Lindaraxas!

An abundant supply of water, brought from the mountains by old Moorish aqueducts, circulates throughout the palace, supplying its baths and fishpools, sparkling in jets within its halls, or murmuring in channels along the marble pavements. When it has paid its tribute to the royal pile, and visited its gardens and parterres, it flows down the long avenue leading to the city, tinkling in rills, gushing in fountains, and maintaining a perpetual verdure in those groves that embower and beautify the whole hill of the Alhambra.

Those only who have sojourned in the ardent climates of the South, can appreciate the delights of an abode, combining the breezy coolness of the mountain with the freshness and verdure of the valley. While the city below pants with the noontide heat, and the parched Vega trembles to the eye, the delicate airs from the Sierra Nevada play through these lofty halls, bringing with them the sweetness of the surrounding gardens. Every thing invites to that indolent repose, the bliss of southern climes; and while the half-shut eye looks out from shaded balconies upon the glittering landscape, the ear is lulled by the rustling of groves, and the murmur of running streams.

I forbear for the present, however, to describe the other delightful apartments of the palace. My object is merely to give the reader a general introduction into an abode where, if so disposed, he may linger and loiter with me day by day until we gradually become familiar with all its localities.

Note on Morisco Architecture

To an unpractised eye the light relievos and fanciful arabesques which cover the walls of the Alhambra appear to have been sculptured by the hand, with a minute and patient labor, an inexhaustible variety of detail, yet a general uniformity and harmony of design truly astonishing; and this may especially be said of the vaults and cupolas, which are wrought like honey-combs, or frostwork, with stalactites and pendants which confound the beholder with the seeming intricacy of their patterns. The astonishment ceases, however, when it is discovered that this is all stucco-work: plates of plaster of Paris, cast in moulds and skilfully joined so as to form patterns of every size and form. This mode of diapering walls with arabesques and stuccoing the vaults with grotto-work, was invented in Damascus, but highly improved by the Moors in Morocco, to whom Saracenic architecture owes its most graceful and fanciful details. The process by which all this fairy tracery was produced was ingeniously simple: The wall in its naked state was divided off by lines crossing at right angles, such as artists use in copying a picture; over these were drawn a succession of intersecting segments of circles. By the aid of these the artists could work with celerity and certainty, and from the mere intersection of the plain and curved lines arose the interminable variety of patterns and the general uniformity of their character.

Much gilding was used in the stucco-work, especially of the cupolas: and the interstices were delicately pencilled with brilliant colors, such as vermilion and lapis lazuli, laid on with the whites of eggs. The primitive colors alone were used, says Ford, by the Egyptians, Greeks, and Arabs, in the early period of art; and they prevail in the Alhambra whenever the artist has been Arabic or Moorish. It is remarkable how much of their original brilliancy remains after the lapse of several centuries.

The lower part of the walls in the saloons, to the height of several feet, is incrusted with glazed tiles, joined like the plates of stucco-work, so as to form various patterns. On some of them are emblazoned the escutcheons of the Moslem kings, traversed with a band and motto. These glazed tiles (azulejos in Spanish, az-zulaj in Arabic) are of Oriental origin; their coolness, cleanliness, and freedom from vermin, render them admirably fitted in sultry climates for paving halls and fountains, incrusting bathing rooms, and lining the walls of chambers. Ford is inclined to give them great antiquity. From their prevailing colors, sapphire and blue, he deduces that they may have formed the kind of pavements alluded to in the sacred Scriptures —"There was under his feet as it were a paved work of a sapphire stone" (Exod. xxiv. 10); and again, "Behold I will lay thy stones with fair colors, and lay thy foundations with sapphires." (Isaiah liv. 11.)

These glazed or porcelain tiles were introduced into Spain at an early date by the Moslems. Some are to be seen among the Moorish ruins which have been there upwards of eight centuries. Manufactures of them still exist in the peninsula, and they are much used in the best Spanish houses, especially in the southern provinces, for paving and lining the summer apartments.

The Spaniards introduced them into the Netherlands when they had possession of that country. The people of Holland adopted them with avidity, as wonderfully suited to their passion for household cleanliness; and thus these Oriental inventions, the azulejos of the Spanish, the az-zulaj of the Arabs, have come to be commonly known as Dutch tiles.

Important Negotiations.
The Author Succeeds to the
Throne of Boabdil

THE DAY was nearly spent before we could tear ourselves from this region of poetry and romance to descend to the city and return to the forlorn realities of a Spanish posada. In a visit of ceremony to the Governor of the Alhambra, to whom we had brought letters, we dwelt with enthusiasm on the scenes we had witnessed, and could not but express surprise that he should reside in the city when he had such a paradise at his command. He pleaded the inconvenience of a residence in the palace from its situation on the crest of a hill, distant from the seat of business and the resorts of social intercourse. It did very well for monarchs, who often had need of castle walls to defend them from their own subjects. "But senores," added he, smiling, "if you think a residence there so desirable, my apartments in the Alhambra are at your service."

It is a common and almost indispensable point of politeness in a Spaniard, to tell you his house is yours. —"Esta casa es siempre a la disposicion de Vm." "This house is always at the command of your Grace." In fact, any thing of his which you admire, is immediately offered to you. It is equally a mark of good breeding in you not to accept it; so we merely bowed our acknowledgments of the courtesy of the Governor in offering us a royal palace. We were mistaken, however. The Governor was in earnest. "You will find a rambling set of empty, unfurnished rooms," said he; "but Tia Antonia, who has charge of the palace, may be able to put them in some kind of order; and to take care of you while you are there. If you can make any arrangement with her for your accommodation, and are content with scanty fare in a royal abode, the palace of King Chico is at your service."

We took the Governor at his word, and hastened up the steep Calle de los Gomeres, and through the Great Gate of Justice, to negotiate with Dame Antonia; doubting at times if this were not a dream, and fearing at times that the sage Duena of the fortress might be slow to capitulate. We knew we had one friend at least in the garrison, who would be in our favor, the bright-eyed little Dolores, whose good graces we had propitiated on our first visit, and who hailed our return to the palace with her brightest looks.

All, however, went smoothly. The good Tia Antonia had a little furniture to put in the rooms, but it was of the commonest kind. We assured her we could bivouac on the floor. She could supply our table, but only in her own simple way — we wanted nothing better. Her niece, Dolores, would wait upon us and at the word we threw up our hats and the bargain was complete.

The very next day we took up our abode in the palace, and never did sovereigns share a divided throne with more perfect harmony. Several days passed by like a dream, when my worthy associate, being summoned to Madrid on diplomatic duties, was compelled to abdicate, leaving me sole monarch of this shadowy realm. For myself, being in a manner a haphazard loiterer about the world and prone to linger in its pleasant places, here have I been suffering day by day to steal away unheeded, spellbound, for aught I know, in this old enchanted pile. Having always a companionable feeling for my reader, and being prone to live with him on confidential terms, I shall make it a point to communicate to him my reveries and researches during this state of delicious thraldom. If they have the power of imparting to his imagination any of the witching charms of the place, he will not repine at lingering with me for a season in the legendary halls of the Alhambra.

At first it is proper to give him some idea of my domestic arrangements; they are rather of a simple kind for the occupant of a regal palace; but I trust they will be less liable to disastrous reverses than those of my royal predecessors.

My quarters are at one end of the Governor's apartment, a suite of empty chambers, in front of the palace, looking out upon the great esplanade called la plaza de los algibes (the place of the cisterns); the apartment is modern, but the end opposite to my sleeping-room communicates with a cluster of little chambers, partly Moorish, partly Spanish, allotted to the chatelaine Dona Antonia and her family. In consideration of keeping the palace in order, the good dame is allowed all the perquisites received from visitors, and all the produce of the gardens; excepting that she is expected to pay an occasional tribute of fruits and flowers to the Governor. Her family consists of a nephew and niece, the children of two different brothers. The nephew, Manuel Molina, is a young man of sterling worth and Spanish gravity. He had served in the army, both in Spain and the West Indies, but is now studying medicine in the hope of one day or other becoming physician to the fortress, a post worth at least one hundred and forty dollars a year. The niece is the plump little black-eyed Dolores already mentioned; and who, it is said, will one day inherit all her aunt's possessions, consisting of certain petty tenements in the fortress, in a somewhat ruinous condition it is true, but which, I am privately assured by Mateo Ximenes, yield a revenue of nearly one hundred and fifty dollars; so that she is quite an heiress in the eyes of the ragged son of the Alhambra. I am also informed by the same observant and authentic personage, that a quiet courtship is going on between the discreet Manuel and his bright-eyed cousin, and that nothing is wanting to enable them to join their hands and expectations but his doctor's diploma, and a dispensation from the Pope on account of their consanguinity.

The good dame Antonia fulfils faithfully her contract in regard to my board and lodging; and as I am easily pleased, I find my fare excellent; while the merry-hearted little Dolores keeps my apartment in order, and officiates as handmaid at meal-times. I have also at my command a tall, stuttering, yellow-haired lad, named Pepe, who works in the gardens, and would fain have acted as valet; but, in this, he was forestalled by Mateo Ximenes, "the son of the Alhambra." This alert and officious wight has managed, somehow or other, to stick by me ever since I first encountered him at the outer gate of the fortress, and to weave himself into all my plans, until he has fairly appointed and installed himself my valet, cicerone, guide, guard, and historio-graphic squire; and I have been obliged to improve the state of his wardrobe, that he may not disgrace his various functions; so that he has cast his old brown mantle, as a snake does his skin, and now appears about the fortress with a smart Andalusian hat and jacket, to his infinite satisfaction, and the great astonishment of his comrades. The chief fault of honest Mateo is an over-anxiety to be useful. Conscious of having foisted himself into my employ, and that my simple and quiet habits render his situation a sinecure, he is at his wit's ends to devise modes of making himself important to my welfare. I am, in a manner, the victim of his officiousness; I cannot put my foot over the threshold of the palace, to stroll about the fortress, but he is at my elbow, to explain every thing I see; and if I venture to ramble among the surrounding hills, he insists upon attending me as a guard, though I vehemently suspect he would be more apt to trust to the length of his legs than the strength of his arms, in case of attack. After all, however, the poor fellow is at times an amusing companion; he is simple-minded, and of infinite good humor, with the loquacity and gossip of a village barber, and knows all the small-talk of the place and its environs; but what he chiefly values himself on, is his stock of local information, having the most marvellous stories to relate of every tower, and vault, and gateway of the fortress, in all of which he places the most implicit faith.

Most of these he has derived, according to his own account, from his grandfather, a little legendary tailor, who lived to the age of nearly a hundred years, during which he made but two migrations beyond the precincts of the fortress. His shop, for the greater part of a century, was the resort of a knot of venerable gossips, where they would pass half the night talking about old times, and the wonderful events and hidden secrets of the place. The whole living, moving, thinking, and acting, of this historical little tailor, had thus been bounded by the walls of the Alhambra; within them he had been born, within them he lived, breathed, and had his being; within them he died, and was buried. Fortunately for posterity, his traditionary lore died not with him. The authentic Mateo, when an urchin, used to be an attentive listener to the narratives of his grandfather, and of the gossip group assembled round the shopboard; and is thus possessed of a stock of valuable knowledge concerning the Alhambra, not to be found in books, and well worthy the attention of every curious traveller.

Such are the personages that constitute my regal household; and I question whether any of the potentates, Moslem or Christian, who have preceded me in the palace, have been waited upon with greater fidelity, or enjoyed a serener sway.

When I rise in the morning, Pepe, the stuttering lad from the gardens, brings me a tribute of fresh culled flowers, which are afterwards arranged in vases, by the skilful hand of Dolores, who takes a female pride in the decorations of my chamber. My meals are made wherever caprice dictates; sometimes in one of the Moorish halls, sometimes under the arcades of the Court of Lions, surrounded by flowers and fountains: and when I walk out, I am conducted by the assiduous Mateo, to the most romantic retreats of the mountains, and delicious haunts of the adjacent valleys, not one of which but is the scene of some wonderful tale.

Though fond of passing the greater part of my day alone, yet I occasionally repair in the evenings to the little domestic circle of Dona Antonia. This is generally held in an old Moorish chamber, which serves the good dame for parlor, kitchen and hall of audience, and which must have boasted of some splendor in the time of the

Moors, if we may judge from the traces yet remaining; but a rude fireplace has been made in modern times in one corner, the smoke from which has discolored the walls, and almost obliterated the ancient arabesques. A window, with a balcony overhanging the valley of the Darro, lets in the cool evening breeze; and here I take my frugal supper of fruit and milk, and mingle with the conversation of the family. There is a natural talent or mother wit, as it is called, about the Spaniards, which renders them intellectual and agreeable companions, whatever may be their condition in life, or however imperfect may have been their education: add to this, they are never vulgar; nature has endowed them with an inherent dignity of spirit. The good Tia Antonia is a woman of strong and intelligent, though uncultivated mind; and the bright-eyed Dolores, though she has read but three or four books in the whole course of her life, has an engaging mixture of naivete and good sense, and often surprises me by the pungency of her artless sallies. Sometimes the nephew entertains us by reading some old comedy of Calderon or Lope de Vega, to which he is evidently prompted by a desire to improve, as well as amuse his cousin Dolores; though, to his great mortification, the little damsel generally falls asleep before the first act is completed. Sometimes Tia Antonia has a little levee of humble friends and dependents, the inhabitants of the adjacent hamlet, or the wives of the invalid soldiers. These look up to her with great deference, as the custodian of the palace, and pay their court to her by bringing the news of the place, or the rumors that may have straggled up from Granada. In listening to these evening gossipings I have picked up many curious facts, illustrative of the manners of the people and the peculiarities of the neighborhood.

These are simple details of simple pleasures; it is the nature of the place alone that gives them interest and importance. I tread haunted ground, and am surrounded by romantic associations. From earliest boyhood, when, on the banks of the Hudson, I first pored over the pages of old Gines Perez de Hytas's apocryphal but chivalresque history of the civil wars of Granada, and the feuds of its gallant cavaliers, the Zegries and Abencerrages, that city has ever been a subject of my waking dreams, and often have I trod in fancy the romantic halls of the Alhambra. Behold for once a day-dream realized; yet I can scarce credit my senses, or believe that I do indeed inhabit the palace of Boabdil, and look down from its balconies upon chivalric Granada. As I loiter through these Oriental chambers, and hear the murmur of fountains and the song of the nightingale; as I inhale the odor of the rose, and feel the influence of the balmy climate, I am almost tempted to fancy myself in the paradise of Mahomet, and that the plump little Dolores is one of the bright-eyed houris, destined to administer to the happiness of true believers.

Inhabitants of the Alhambra

I have often observed that the more proudly a mansion has been tenanted in the day of its prosperity, the humbler are its inhabitants in the day of its decline, and that the palace of a king commonly ends in being the nestling-place of the beggar.

The Alhambra is in a rapid state of similar transition. Whenever a tower falls to decay, it is seized upon by some tatterdemalion family, who become joint-tenants, with the bats and owls, of its gilded halls, and hang their rags, those standards of poverty, out of its windows and loopholes.

I have amused myself with remarking some of the motley characters that have thus usurped the ancient abode of royalty, and who seem as if placed here to give a farcical termination to the drama of human pride. One of these even bears the mockery of a regal title. It is a little old woman named Maria Antonia Sabonea, but who goes by the appellation of la Reyna Coquina, or the Cockle-queen. She is small enough to be a fairy, and a fairy she may be for aught I can find out, for no one seems to know her origin. Her habitation is in a kind of closet under the outer staircase of the palace, and she sits in the cool stone corridor, plying her needle and singing from morning till night, with a ready joke for every one that passes; for though one of the poorest, she is one of the merriest little women breathing. Her great merit is a gift for story-telling, having, I verily believe, as many stories at her command, as the inexhaustible Scheherezade of the thousand and one nights. Some of these I have heard her relate in the evening tertulias of Dame Antonia, at which she is occasionally a humble attendant.

That there must be some fairy gift about this mysterious little old woman, would appear from her extraordinary luck, since, notwithstanding her being very little, very ugly, and very poor, she has had, according to her own account, five husbands and a half, reckoning as a half one a young dragoon, who died during courtship. A rival personage to this little fairy queen is a portly old fellow with a bottle-nose, who goes about in a rusty garb with a cocked hat of oil-skin and a red cockade. He is one of the legitimate sons of the Alhambra, and has lived here all his life, filling various offices, such as deputy alguazil, sexton of the parochial church, and marker of a fives-court established at the foot of one of the towers. He is as poor as a rat, but as proud as he is ragged, boasting of his descent from the illustrious house of Aguilar, from which sprang Gonzalvo of Cordova, the grand captain. Nay, he actually bears the name of Alonzo de Aguilar, so renowned in the history of the conquest; though the graceless wags of the fortress have given him the title of el padre santo, or the holy father, the usual appellation of the Pope, which I had thought too sacred in the eyes of true Catholics to be thus ludicrously applied. It is a whimsical caprice of fortune to present, in the grotesque person of this tatterdemalion, a namesake and descendant of the proud Alonzo de Aguilar, the mirror of Andalusian chivalry, leading an almost mendicant existence about this once haughty fortress, which his ancestor aided to reduce; yet, such might have been the lot of the descendants of Agamemnon and Achilles, had they lingered about the ruins of Troy!

Of this motley community, I find the family of my gossiping squire, Mateo Ximenes, to form, from their numbers at least, a very important part. His boast of being a son of the Alhambra, is not unfounded. His family has inhabited the fortress ever since the time of the conquest, handing down an hereditary poverty from father to son; not one of them having ever been known to be worth a maravedi. His father, by trade a ribbon-weaver, and who succeeded the historical tailor as the head of the family, is now near seventy years of age, and lives in a hovel of reeds and plaster, built by his own hands, just above the iron gate. The furniture consists of a crazy bed, a table, and two or three chairs; a wooden chest, containing, besides his scanty clothing, the "archives of the family." These are nothing more nor less than the papers of various lawsuits sustained by different generations; by which it would seem that, with all their apparent carelessness and good humor, they are a litigious brood. Most of the suits have been brought against gossiping neighbors for questioning the purity of their blood, and denying their being Cristianos viejos, i. e. old Christians, without Jewish or Moorish taint. In fact, I doubt whether this jealousy about their blood has not kept them so poor in purse: spending all their earnings on escribanos and alguazils. The pride of the hovel is an escutcheon suspended against the wall, in which are emblazoned quarterings of the arms of the Marquis of Caiesedo, and of various other noble houses, with which this poverty-stricken brood claim affinity.

As to Mateo himself, who is now about thirty-five years of age, he has done his utmost to perpetuate his line and continue the poverty of the family, having a wife and a numerous progeny, who inhabit an almost dismantled hovel in the hamlet. How they manage to subsist, he only who sees into all mysteries can tell; the subsistence of a Spanish family of the kind, is always a riddle to me; yet they do subsist, and what is more, appear to enjoy their existence. The wife takes her holiday stroll on the Paseo of Granada, with a child in her arms and half a dozen at her heels; and the eldest daughter, now verging into womanhood, dresses her hair with flowers, and dances gayly to the castanets.

There are two classes of people to whom life seems one long holiday, the very rich, and the very poor; one because they need do nothing, the other because they have nothing to do; but there are none who understand the art of doing nothing and living upon nothing, better than the poor classes of Spain. Climate does one half, and temperament the rest. Give a Spaniard the shade in summer, and the sun in winter; a little bread, garlic, oil, and garbances, an old brown cloak and a guitar, and let the world roll on as it pleases. Talk of poverty! with him it has no disgrace. It sits upon him with a grandiose style, like his ragged cloak. He is a hidalgo, even when in rags.

The "sons of the Alhambra" are an eminent illustration of this practical philosophy. As the Moors imagined that the celestial paradise hung over this favored spot, so I am inclined at times to fancy, that a gleam of the golden age still lingers about this ragged community. They possess nothing, they do nothing, they care for nothing. Yet, though apparently idle all the week, they are as observant of all holy days and saints' days as the most laborious artisan. They attend all fetes and dancings in Granada and its vicinity, light bonfires on the hills on St. John's eve, and dance away the moonlight nights on the harvest-home of a small field within the precincts of the fortress, which yields a few bushels of wheat.

Before concluding these remarks, I must mention one of the amusements of the place which has particularly struck me. I had repeatedly observed a long lean fellow perched on the top of one of the towers, manoeuvring two or three fishing-rods, as though he were angling for the stars. I was for some time perplexed by the evolutions of this aerial fisherman, and my perplexity increased on observing others employed in like manner on different parts of the battlements and bastions; it was not until I consulted Mateo Ximenes, that I solved the mystery.

It seems that the pure and airy situation of this fortress has rendered it, like the castle of Macbeth, a prolific breeding-place for swallows and martlets, who sport about its towers in myriads, with the holiday glee of urchins just let loose from school. To entrap these birds in their giddy circlings, with hooks baited with flies, is one of the favorite amusements of the ragged "sons of the Alhambra," who, with the good-for-nothing ingenuity of arrant idlers, have thus invented the art of angling in the sky.

The Hall of Ambassadors

In one of my visits to the old Moorish chamber, where the good Tia Antonia cooks her dinner and receives her company, I observed a mysterious door in one corner, leading apparently into the ancient part of the edifice. My curiosity being aroused, I opened it, and found myself in a narrow, blind corridor, groping along which I came to the head of a dark winding staircase, leading down an angle of the Tower of Comares. Down this staircase I descended darkling, guiding myself by the wall until I came to a small door at the bottom, throwing which open, I was suddenly dazzled by emerging into the brilliant antechamber of the Hall of Ambassadors; with the fountain of the Court of the Alberca sparkling before me. The antechamber is separated from the court by an elegant gallery, supported by slender columns with spandrels of open work in the Morisco style. At each end of the antechamber are alcoves, and its ceiling is richly stuccoed and painted. Passing through a magnificent portal I found myself in the far-famed Hall of Ambassadors, the audience chamber of the Moslem monarchs. It is said to be thirty-seven feet square, and sixty feet high; occupies the whole interior of the Tower of Comares; and still bears the traces of past magnificence. The walls are beautifully stuccoed and decorated with Morisco fancifulness; the lofty ceiling was originally of the same favorite material, with the usual frostwork and pensile ornaments or stalactites; which, with the embellishments of vivid coloring and gilding, must have been gorgeous in the extreme. Unfortunately it gave way during an earthquake, and brought down with it an immense arch which traversed the hall. It was replaced by the present vault or dome of larch or cedar, with intersecting ribs, the whole curiously wrought and richly colored; still Oriental in its character, reminding one of "those ceilings of cedar and vermilion that we read of in the prophets and the Arabian Nights."*

* Urquhart's Pillars of Hercules.

From the great height of the vault above the windows the upper part of the hall is almost lost in obscurity; yet there is a magnificence as well as solemnity in the gloom, as through it we have gleams of rich gilding and the brilliant tints of the Moorish pencil.

The royal throne was placed opposite the entrance in a recess, which still bears an inscription intimating that Yusef I (the monarch who completed the Alhambra) made this the throne of his empire. Every thing in this noble hall seems to have been calculated to surround the throne with impressive dignity and splendor; there was none of the elegant voluptuousness which reigns in other parts of the palace. The tower is of massive strength, domineering over the whole edifice and overhanging the steep hillside. On three sides of the Hall of Ambassadors are windows cut through the immense thickness of the walls, and commanding extensive prospects. The balcony of the central window especially looks down upon the verdant valley of the Darro, with its walks, its groves, and gardens. To the left it enjoys a distant prospect of the Vega, while directly in front rises the rival height of the Albaycin, with its medley of streets, and terraces, and gardens, and once crowned by a fortress that vied in power with the Alhambra. "Ill fated the man who lost all this!" exclaimed Charles V, as he looked forth from this window upon the enchanting scenery it commands.

The balcony of the window where this royal exclamation was made, has of late become one of my favorite resorts. I have just been seated there, enjoying the close of a long brilliant day. The sun, as he sank behind the purple mountains of Alhama, sent a stream of effulgence up the valley of the Darro, that spread a melancholy pomp over the ruddy towers of the Alhambra; while the Vega, covered with a slight sultry vapor that caught the setting ray, seemed spread out in the distance like a golden sea. Not a breath of air disturbed the stillness of the hour, and though the faint sound of music and merriment now and then rose from the gardens of the Darro, it but rendered more impressive the monumental silence of the pile which overshadowed me. It was one of those hours and scenes in which memory asserts an almost magical power; and, like the evening sun beaming on these mouldering towers, sends back her retrospective rays to light up the glories of the past.

As I sat watching the effect of the declining daylight upon this Moorish pile, I was led into a consideration of the light, elegant, and voluptuous character, prevalent throughout its internal architecture; and to contrast it with the grand but gloomy solemnity of the Gothic edifices reared by the Spanish conquerors. The very architecture thus bespeaks the opposite and irreconcilable natures of the two warlike people who so long battled here for the mastery of the peninsula. By degrees, I fell into a course of musing upon the singular fortunes of the Arabian or Morisco-Spaniards, whose whole existence is as a tale that is told, and certainly forms one of the most anomalous yet splendid episodes in history. Potent and durable as was their dominion, we scarcely know how to call them. They were a nation without a legitimate country or name. A remote wave of the great Arabian inundation, cast upon the shores of Europe, they seem to have all the impetus of the first rush of the torrent. Their career of conquest, from the rock of Gibraltar to the cliffs of the Pyrenees, was as rapid and brilliant as the Moslem victories of Syria and Egypt. Nay, had they not been checked on the plains of Tours, all France, all Europe, might have been overrun with the same facility as the empires of the East, and the crescent at this day have glittered on the fanes of Paris and London.

Repelled within the limits of the Pyrenees, the mixed hordes of Asia and Africa, that formed this great irruption, gave up the Moslem principle of conquest, and sought to establish in Spain a peaceful and permanent dominion. As conquerors, their heroism was only equalled by their moderation; and in both, for a time, they excelled the nations with whom they contended. Severed from their native homes, they loved the land given them as they supposed by Allah, and strove to embellish it with every thing that could administer to the happiness of man. Laying the foundations of their power in a system of wise and equitable laws, diligently cultivating the arts and sciences, and promoting agriculture, manufactures, and commerce; they gradually formed an empire unrivalled for its prosperity by any of the empires of Christendom; and diligently drawing round them the graces and refinements which marked the Arabian empire in the East, at the time of its greatest civilization, they diffused the light of Oriental knowledge, through the Western regions of benighted Europe.

The cities of Arabian Spain became the resort of Christian artisans, to instruct themselves in the useful arts. The universities of Toledo, Cordova, Seville, and Granada, were sought by the pale student from other lands to acquaint himself with the sciences of the Arabs, and the treasured lore of antiquity; the lovers of the gay science, resorted to Cordova and Granada, to imbibe the poetry and music of the East; and the steel-clad warriors of the North hastened thither to accomplish themselves in the graceful exercises and courteous usages of chivalry.

If the Moslem monuments in Spain, if the Mosque of Cordova, the Alcazar of Seville, and the Alhambra of Granada, still bear inscriptions fondly boasting of the power and permanency of their dominion; can the boast be derided as arrogant and vain? Generation after generation, century after century, passed away, and still they maintained possession of the land. A period elapsed longer than that which has passed since England was subjugated by the Norman Conqueror, and the descendants of Musa and Taric might as little anticipate being driven into exile across the same straits, traversed by their triumphant ancestors, as the descendants of Rollo and William, and their veteran peers, may dream of being driven back to the shores of Normandy.

With all this, however, the Moslem empire in Spain was but a brilliant exotic, that took no permanent root in the soil it embellished. Severed from all their neighbors in the West, by impassable barriers of faith and manners, and separated by seas and deserts from their kindred of the East, the Morisco-spaniards were an isolated people. Their whole existence was a prolonged, though gallant and chivalric struggle, for a foothold in a usurped land.

They were the outposts and frontiers of Islamism. The peninsula was the great battle-ground where the Gothic conquerors of the North and the Moslem conquerors of the East, met and strove for mastery; and the fiery courage of the Arab was at length subdued by the obstinate and persevering valor of the Goth.

Never was the annihilation of a people more complete than that of the Morisco-Spaniards. Where are they? Ask the shores of Barbary and its desert places. The exiled remnant of their once powerful empire disappeared among the barbarians of Africa, and ceased to be a nation. They have not even left a distinct name behind them, though for nearly eight centuries they were a distinct people. The home of their adoption, and of their occupation for ages, refuses to acknowledge them, except as invaders and usurpers. A few broken monuments are all that remain to bear witness to their power and dominion, as solitary rocks, left far in the interior, bear testimony to the extent of some vast inundation. Such is the Alhambra. A Moslem pile in the midst of a Christian land; an Oriental palace amidst the Gothic edifices of the West; an elegant memento of a brave, intelligent, and graceful people, who conquered, ruled, flourished, and passed away.

The Jesuits' Library

Since indulging in the foregoing reverie, my curiosity has been aroused to know something of the princes, who left behind them this monument of Oriental taste and magnificence; and whose names still appear among the inscriptions on its walls. To gratify this curiosity, I have descended from this region of fancy and fable, where every thing is liable to take an imaginary tint, and have carried my researches among the dusty tomes of the old Jesuits' Library, in the University. This once boasted repository of erudition is now a mere shadow of its former self, having been stripped of its manuscripts and rarest works by the French, when masters of Granada; still it contains among many ponderous tomes of the Jesuit fathers, which the French were careful to leave behind, several curious tracts of Spanish literature; and above all, a number of those antiquated parchment-bound chronicles for which I have a particular veneration.

In this old library, I have passed many delightful hours of quiet, undisturbed, literary foraging; for the keys of the doors and bookcases were kindly intrusted to me, and I was left alone, to rummage at my pleasure — a rare indulgence in these sanctuaries of learning, which too often tantalize the thirsty student with the sight of sealed fountains of knowledge.

In the course of these visits I gleaned a variety of facts concerning historical characters connected with the Alhambra, some of which I here subjoin, trusting they may prove acceptable to the reader.

Alhamar The Founder of the Alhambra

The Moors of Granada regarded the Alhambra as a miracle of art, and had a tradition that the king who founded it dealt in magic, or at least in alchemy, by means whereof he procured the immense sums of gold expended in its erection. A brief view of his reign will show the secret of his wealth. He is known in Arabian history as Muhamed Ibn-l-Ahmar; but his name in general is written simply Alhamar, and was given to him, we are told, on account of his ruddy complexion, because his complexion was very ruddy the Moors called him Abenalhamar, which means "vermilion" . . . and because the Moors called him Benalhamar, which means vermilion, he took bright red for his insignia, just as the Kings of Granada have done ever since.

He was of the noble and opulent line of the Beni Nasar, or tribe of Nasar, and was born in Arjona, in the year of the Hegira 592 (A. D. 1195). At his birth the astrologers, we are told, cast his horoscope according to Oriental custom, and pronounced it highly auspicious; and a santon predicted for him a glorious career. No expense was spared in fitting him for the high destinies prognosticated. Before he attained the full years of manhood, the famous battle of the Navas (or plains) of Tolosa shattered the Moorish empire, and eventually severed the Moslems of Spain from the Moslems of Africa. Factions soon arose among the former, headed by warlike chiefs, ambitious of grasping the sovereignty of the Peninsula. Alhamar became engaged in these wars; he was the general and leader of the Beni Nasar, and, as such, he opposed and thwarted the ambition of Aben Hud, who had raised his standard among the warlike mountains of the Alpuxarras, and been proclaimed king of Murcia and Granada. Many conflicts took place between these warring chieftains; Alhamar dispossessed his rival of several important places, and was proclaimed king of Jaen by his soldiery; but he aspired to the sovereignty of the whole of Andalusia, for he was of a sanguine spirit and lofty ambition. His valor and generosity went hand in hand; what he gained by the one he secured by the other; and at the death of Aben Hud (A. D. 1238), he became sovereign of all the territories which owned allegiance to that powerful chief He made his formal entry into Granada in the same year, amid the enthusiastic shouts of the multitude, who hailed him as the only one capable of uniting the various factions which prevailed, and which threatened to lay the empire at the mercy of the Christian princes.

Alhamar established his court in Granada; he was the first of the illustrious line of Nasar that sat upon a throne. He took immediate measures to put his little kingdom in a posture of defence against the assaults to be expected from his Christian neighbors, repairing and strengthening the frontier posts and fortifying the capital. Not content with the provisions of the Moslem law, by which every man is made a soldier, he raised a regular army to garrison his strong-holds, allowing every soldier stationed on the frontier a portion of land for the support of himself, his horse, and his family; thus interesting him in the defence of the soil in which he had a property. These wise precautions were justified by events. The Christians, profiting by the dismemberment of the Moslem power, were rapidly regaining their ancient territories. James the Conqueror had subjected all Valencia, and Ferdinand the Saint sat down in person before Jaen, the bulwark of Granada. Alhamar ventured to oppose him in open field, but met with a signal defeat, and retired discomfited to his capital. Jaen still held out, and kept the enemy at bay during an entire winter, but Ferdinand swore not to raise his camp until he had gained possession of the place. Alhamar found it impossible to throw reinforcements into the besieged city; he saw that its fall must be followed by the investment of his capital, and was conscious of the insufficiency of his means to cope with the potent sovereign of Castile. Taking a sudden resolution, therefore, he repaired privately to the Christian camp, made his unexpected appearance in the presence of King Ferdinand, and frankly announced himself as the king of Granada. "I come," said he, "confiding in your good faith, to put myself under your protection. Take all I possess and receive me as your vassal"; so saying, he knelt and kissed the king's hand in token of allegiance.

Ferdinand was won by this instance of confiding faith, and determined not to be outdone in generosity. He raised his late enemy from the earth, embraced him as a friend, and, refusing the wealth he offered, left him sovereign of his dominions, under the feudal tenure of a yearly tribute, attendance at the Cortes as one of the nobles of the empire, and service in war with a certain number of horsemen. He moreover conferred on him the honor of knighthood, and armed him with his own hands.

It was not long after this that Alhamar was called upon, for his military services, to aid King Ferdinand in his famous siege of Seville. The Moorish king sallied forth with five hundred chosen horsemen of Granada, than whom none in the world knew better how to manage the steed or wield the lance. It was a humiliating service, however, for they had to draw the sword against their brethren of the faith.

Alhamar gained a melancholy distinction by his prowess in this renowned conquest, but more true honor by the humanity which he prevailed upon Ferdinand to introduce into the usages of war. When in 1248 the famous city of Seville surrendered to the Castilian monarch, Alhamar returned sad and full of care to his dominions. He saw the gathering ills that menaced the Moslem cause; and uttered an ejaculation often used by him in moments of anxiety and trouble — "How straitened and wretched would be our life, if our hope were not so spacious and extensive." "Que angosta y miserable seria nuestra vida, sino fuera tan dilatada y espaciosa nuestra esperanza!"

As he approached Granada on his return he beheld arches of triumph which had been erected in honor of his martial exploits. The people thronged forth to see him with impatient joy, for his benignant rule had won all hearts. Wherever he passed he was hailed with acclamations as "El Ghalib!" (the conqueror). Alhamar gave a melancholy shake of the head on hearing the appellation. "Wa le ghalib il Allah!" ("There is no conqueror but God!"), exclaimed he. From that time forward this exclamation became his motto, and the motto of his descendants, and appears to this day emblazoned on his escutcheons in the halls of the Alhambra.

Alhamar had purchased peace by submission to the Christian yoke; but he was conscious that, with elements so discordant and motives for hostility so deep and ancient, it could not be permanent. Acting, therefore, upon the old maxim, "arm thyself in peace and clothe thyself in summer," he improved the present interval of tranquillity by fortifying his dominions, replenishing his arsenals, and promoting those useful arts which give wealth and real power. He confided the command of his various cities to such as had distinguished themselves by valor and prudence, and who seemed most acceptable to the people. He organized a vigilant police, and established rigid rules for the administration of justice. The poor and the distressed always found ready admission to his presence, and he attended personally to their assistance and redress. He erected hospitals for the blind, the aged, and infirm, and all those incapable of labor, and visited them frequently; not on set days with pomp and form, so as to give time for every thing to be put in order, and every abuse concealed; but suddenly, and unexpectedly, informing himself, by actual observation and close inquiry, of the treatment of the sick, and the conduct of those appointed to administer to their relief. He founded schools and colleges, which he visited in the same manner, inspecting personally the instruction of the youth. He established butcheries and public ovens, that the people might be furnished with wholesome provisions at just and regular prices. He introduced abundant streams of water into the city, erecting baths and fountains, and constructing aqueducts and canals to irrigate and fertilize the Vega. By these means prosperity and abundance prevailed in this beautiful city, its gates were thronged with commerce, and its warehouses filled with luxuries and merchandise of every clime and country.

He moreover gave premiums and privileges to the best artisans; improved the breed of horses and other domestic animals; encouraged husbandry; and increased the natural fertility of the soil twofold by his protection, making the lovely valleys of his kingdom to bloom like gardens. He fostered also the growth and fabrication of silk, until the looms of Granada surpassed even those of Syria in the fineness and beauty of their productions. He moreover caused the mines of gold and silver and other metals, found in the mountainous regions of his dominions, to be diligently worked, and was the first king of Granada who struck money of gold and silver with his name, taking great care that the coins should be skilfully executed.

It was towards the middle of the thirteenth century, and just after his return from the siege of Seville, that he commenced the splendid palace of the Alhambra; superintending the building of it in person; mingling frequently among the artists and workmen, and directing their labors.

Though thus magnificent in his works and great in his enterprises, he was simple in his person and moderate in his enjoyments. His dress was not merely void of splendor, but so plain as not to distinguish him from his subjects. His harem boasted but few beauties, and these he visited but seldom, though they were entertained with great magnificence. His wives were daughters of the principal nobles, and were treated by him as friends and rational companions. What is more, he managed to make them live in friendship with one another. He passed much of his time in his gardens; especially in those of the Alhambra, which he had stored with the rarest plants and the most beautiful and aromatic flowers. Here he delighted himself in reading histories, or in causing them to be read and related to him, and sometimes, in intervals of leisure, employed himself in the instruction of his three sons, for whom he had provided the most learned and virtuous masters.

As he had frankly and voluntarily offered himself a tributary vassal to Ferdinand, so he always remained loyal to his word, giving him repeated proofs of fidelity and attachment. When that renowned monarch died in Seville in 1254, Alhamar sent ambassadors to condole with his successor, Alonzo X, and with them a gallant train of a hundred Moorish cavaliers of distinguished rank, who were to attend round the royal bier during the funeral ceremonies, each bearing a lighted taper. This grand testimonial of respect was repeated by the Moslem monarch during the remainder of his life on each anniversary of the death of King Ferdinand el Santo, when the hundred Moorish knights repaired from Granada to Seville, and took their stations with lighted tapers in the centre of the sumptuous cathedral round the cenotaph of the illustrious deceased.

Alhamar retained his faculties and vigor to an advanced age. In his seventy-ninth year (A. D. 1272) he took the field on horseback, accompanied by the flower of his chivalry, to resist an invasion of his territories. As the army sallied forth from Granada, one of the principal adalides, or guides, who rode in the advance, accidentally broke his lance against the arch of the gate. The councillors of the king, alarmed by this circumstance, which was considered an evil omen, entreated him to return. Their supplications were in vain. The king persisted, and at noontide the omen, say the Moorish chroniclers, was fatally fulfilled. Alhamar was suddenly struck with illness, and had nearly fallen from his horse. He was placed on a litter, and borne back towards Granada but his illness increased to such a degree that they were obliged to pitch his tent in the Vega. His physicians were filled with consternation, not knowing what remedy to prescribe. In a few hours he died, vomiting blood and in violent convulsions. The Castilian prince, Don Philip, brother of Alonzo X, was by his side when he expired. His body was embalmed, enclosed in a silver coffin, and buried in the Alhambra in a sepulchre of precious marble, amidst the unfeigned lamentations of his subjects, who bewailed him as a parent.

I have said that he was the first of the illustrious line of Nasar that sat upon a throne. I may add that he was the founder of a brilliant kingdom, which will ever be famous in history and romance, as the last rallying place, of Moslem power and splendor in the peninsula. Though his undertakings were vast, and his expenditures immense, yet his treasury was always full; and this seeming contradiction gave rise to the story that he was versed in magic art, and possessed of the secret for transmuting baser metals into gold. Those who have attended to his domestic policy, as here set forth, will easily understand the natural magic and simple alchemy which made his ample treasury to overflow.

Yusef Abul Hagig, The Finisher of the Alhambra

To the foregoing particulars, concerning the Moslem princes who once reigned in these halls, I shall add a brief notice of the monarch who completed and embellished the Alhambra. Yusef Abul Hagig (or as it is sometimes written, Haxis) was another prince of the noble line of Nasar. He ascended the throne of Granada in the year of grace 1333, and is described by Moslem writers as having a noble presence, great bodily strength, and a fair complexion, and the majesty of his countenance increased, say they, by suffering his beard to grow to a dignified length and dying it black. His manners were gentle, affable, and urbane; he carried the benignity of his nature into warfare, prohibiting all wanton cruelty, and enjoining mercy and protection towards women and children, the aged and infirm, and all friars and other persons of holy and recluse life. But though he possessed the courage common to generous spirits, the bent of his genius was more for peace than war, and though repeatedly obliged by circumstances to take up arms, he was generally unfortunate.

Among other ill-starred enterprises, he undertook a great campaign, in conjunction with the king of Morocco, against the kings of Castile and Portugal, but was defeated in the memorable battle of Salado, which had nearly proved a death-blow to the Moslem power in Spain.

Yusef obtained a long truce after this defeat, and now his character shone forth in its true lustre. He had an excellent memory, and had stored his mind with science and erudition; his taste was altogether elegant and refined, and he was accounted the best poet of his time. Devoting himself to the instruction of his people and the improvement of their morals and manners, he established schools in all the villages, with simple and uniform systems of education; he obliged every hamlet of more than twelve houses to have a mosque, and purified the ceremonies of religion, and the festivals and popular amusements, from various abuses and indecorums which had crept into them. He attended vigilantly to the police of the city, establishing nocturnal guards and patrols, and superintending all municipal concerns. His attention was also directed towards finishing the great architectural works commenced by his predecessors, and erecting others on his own plans. The Alhambra, which had been founded by the good Alhamar, was now completed. Yusef constructed the beautiful Gate of Justice, forming the grand entrance to the fortress, which he finished in 1348. He likewise adorned many of the courts and halls of the palace, as may be seen by the inscriptions on the walls, in which his name repeatedly occurs. He built also the noble Alcazar or citadel of Malaga, now unfortunately a mere mass of crumbling ruins, but which most probably exhibited in its interior, similar elegance and magnificence with the Alhambra.

The genius of a sovereign stamps a character upon his time. The nobles of Granada, imitating the elegant and graceful taste of Yusef, soon filled the city of Granada with magnificent palaces; the halls of which were paved with mosaic, the walls and ceilings wrought in fretwork, and delicately gilded and painted with azure, vermilion, and other brilliant colors, or minutely inlaid with cedar and other precious woods; specimens of which have survived, in all their lustre, the lapse of several centuries. Many of the houses had fountains, which threw up jets of water to refresh and cool the air. They had lofty towers also, of wood or stone, curiously carved and ornamented, and covered with plates of metal that glittered in the sun. Such was the refined and delicate taste in architecture that prevailed among this elegant people; insomuch that to use the beautiful simile of an Arabian writer, "Granada, in the days of Yusef, was as a silver vase filled with emeralds and jacinths."

One anecdote will be sufficient to show the magnanimity of this generous prince. The long truce which had succeeded the battle of Salado was at an end, and every effort of Yusef to renew it was in vain. His deadly foe, Alfonzo XI of Castile, took the field with great force, and laid siege to Gibraltar. Yusef reluctantly took up arms, and sent troops to the relief of the place. In the midst of his anxiety, he received tidings that his dreaded foe had suddenly fallen a victim to the plague. Instead of manifesting exultation on the occasion, Yusef called to mind the great qualities of the deceased, and was touched with a noble sorrow. "Alas!" cried he, "the world has lost one of its most excellent princes; a sovereign who knew how to honor merit, whether in friend or foe!"

The Spanish chroniclers themselves bear witness to this magnanimity. According to their accounts, the Moorish cavaliers partook of the sentiment of their king, and put on mourning for the death of Alfonzo. Even those of Gibraltar, who had been so closely invested, when they knew that the hostile monarch lay dead in his camp, determined among themselves that no hostile movement should be made against the Christians. The day on which the camp was broken up, and the army departed bearing the corpse of Alfonzo, the Moors issued in multitudes from Gibraltar, and stood mute and melancholy, watching the mournful pageant. The same reverence for the deceased was observed by all the Moorish commanders on the frontiers, who suffered the funeral train to pass in safety, bearing the corpse of the Christian sovereign from Gibraltar to Seville.

And the Moors that were in the city and Castle of Gibraltar, after they knew that King Don Alonzo was dead, ordered among themselves that no one should dare to make any move against the Christians, nor to start fighting against them, and they all remained quiet and told each other that on that day had died a noble king and a great prince of the world.

Yusef did not long survive the enemy he had so generously deplored. In the year 1354, as he was one day praying in the royal mosque of the Alhambra, a maniac rushed suddenly from behind and plunged a dagger in his side. The cries of the king brought his guards and courtiers to his assistance. They found him weltering in his blood. He made some signs as if to speak, but his words were unintelligible. They bore him senseless to the royal apartments, where he expired almost immediately. The murderer was cut to pieces, and his limbs burnt in public to gratify the fury of the populace.

The body of the king was interred in a superb sepulchre of white marble; a long epitaph, in letters of gold upon an azure ground, recorded his virtues. "Here lies a king and martyr, of an illustrious line, gentle, learned, and virtuous; renowned for the graces of his person and his manners; whose clemency, piety and benevolence, were extolled throughout the kingdom of Granada. He was a great prince; an illustrious captain; a sharp sword of the Moslems; a valiant standard-bearer among the most potent monarchs," &c.

The mosque still exists which once resounded with the dying cries of Yusef, but the monument which recorded his virtues has long since disappeared. His name, however, remains inscribed among the delicate and graceful ornaments of the Alhambra, and will be perpetuated in connection with this renowned pile, which it was his pride and delight to beautify.

Washington Irving

The Mysterious Chambers

As I was rambling one day about the Moorish halls, my attention was, for the first time, attracted to a door in a remote gallery, communicating apparently with some part of the Alhambra which I had not yet explored. I attempted to open it, but it was locked. I knocked, but no one answered, and the sound seemed to reverberate through empty chambers. Here then was a mystery. Here was the haunted wing of the castle. How was I to get at the dark secrets here shut up from the public eye? Should I come privately at night with lamp and sword, according to the prying custom of heroes of romance; or should I endeavor to draw the secret from Pepe the stuttering gardener; or the ingenuous Dolores, or the loquacious Mateo? Or should I go frankly and openly to Dame Antonia the chatelaine, and ask her all about it? I chose the latter course, as being the simplest though the least romantic; and found, somewhat to my disappointment, that there was no mystery in the case. I was welcome to explore the apartment, and there was the key.

Thus provided, I returned forthwith to the door. It opened, as I had surmised, to a range of vacant chambers; but they were quite different from the rest of the palace. The architecture, though rich and antiquated, was European. There was nothing Moorish about it. The first two rooms were lofty; the ceilings, broken in many places, were of cedar, deeply panelled and skilfully carved with fruits and flowers, intermingled with grotesque masks or faces.

The walls had evidently in ancient times been hung with damask; but now were naked, and scrawled over by that class of aspiring travellers who defile noble monuments with their worthless names. The windows, dismantled and open to wind and weather, looked out into a charming little secluded garden, where an alabaster fountain sparkled among roses and myrtles, and was surrounded by orange and citron trees, some of which flung their branches into the chambers. Beyond these rooms were two saloons, longer but less lofty, looking also into the garden. In the compartments of the panelled ceilings were baskets of fruit and garlands of flowers, painted by no mean hand, and in tolerable preservation. The walls also had been painted in fresco in the Italian style, but the paintings were nearly obliterated; the windows were in the same shattered state with those of the other chambers. This fanciful suite of rooms terminated in an open gallery with balustrades, running at right angles along another side of the garden. The whole apartment, so delicate and elegant in its decorations, so choice and sequestered in its situation along this retired little garden, and so different in architecture from the neighboring halls, awakened an interest in its history. I found on inquiry that it was an apartment fitted up by Italian artists in the early part of the last century, at the time when Philip V and his second wife, the beautiful Elizabetta of Farnese, daughter of the Duke of Parma, were expected at the Alhambra. It was destined for the queen and the ladies of her train. One of the loftiest chambers had been her sleeping room. A narrow staircase, now walled up, led up to a delightful belvidere, originally a mirador of the Moorish sultanas, communicating with the harem; but which was fitted up as a boudoir for the fair Elizabetta, and still retains the name of el tocador de la Reyna, or the queen's toilette.

One window of the royal sleeping-room commanded a prospect of the Generalife and its embowered terraces, another looked out into the little secluded garden I have mentioned, which was decidedly Moorish in its character, and also had its history. It was in fact the garden of Lindaraxa, so often mentioned in descriptions of the Alhambra; but who this Lindaraxa was I have never heard explained. A little research gave me the few particulars known about her. She was a Moorish beauty who flourished in the court of Muhamed the Left-handed, and was the daughter of his loyal adherent, the alcayde of Malaga, who sheltered him in his city when driven from the throne. On regaining his crown, the alcayde was rewarded for his fidelity. His daughter had her apartment in the Alhambra, and was given by the king in marriage to Nasar, a young Cetimerien prince descended from Aben Hud the Just. Their espousals were doubtless celebrated in the royal palace, and their honeymoon may have passed among these very bowers.

One of the things in which the Moorish kings interfered was in the marriage of their nobles: hence it came that all the senores attached to the royal person were married in the palace; and there was always a chamber destined for the ceremony.

Four centuries had elapsed since the fair Lindaraxa passed away, yet how much of the fragile beauty of the scenes she inhabited remained! The garden still bloomed in which she delighted; the fountain still presented the crystal mirror in which her charms may once have been reflected; the alabaster, it is true, had lost its whiteness; the basin beneath, overrun with weeds, had become the lurking-place of the lizard, but there was something in the very decay that enhanced the interest of the scene, speaking as it did of that mutability, the irrevocable lot of man and all his works.

The desolation too of these chambers, once the abode of the proud and elegant Elizabetta, had a more touching charm for me than if I had beheld them in their pristine splendor, glittering with the pageantry of a court.

When I returned to my quarters, in the governor's apartment, every thing seemed tame and common-place after the poetic region I had left. The thought suggested itself: Why could I not change my quarters to these vacant chambers? that would indeed be living in the Alhambra, surrounded by its gardens and fountains, as in the time of the Moorish sovereigns. I proposed the change to Dame Antonia and her family, and it occasioned vast surprise. They could not conceive any rational inducement for the choice of an apartment so forlorn, remote and solitary. Dolores exclaimed at its frightful loneliness; nothing but bats and owls flitting about — and then a fox and wild-cat, kept in the vaults of the neighboring baths, roamed about at night. The good Tia had more reasonable objections. The neighborhood was infested by vagrants; gipsies swarmed in the caverns of the adjacent hills; the palace was ruinous and easy to be entered in many places; the rumor of a stranger quartered alone in one of the remote and ruined apartments, out of the hearing of the rest of the inhabitants, might tempt unwelcome visitors in the night, especially as foreigners were always supposed to be well stocked with money. I was not to be diverted from my humor, however, and my will was law with these good people. So, calling in the assistance of a carpenter, and the ever officious Mateo Ximenes, the doors and windows were soon placed in a state of tolerable security, and the sleeping-room of the stately Elizabetta prepared for my reception. Mateo kindly volunteered as a body-guard to sleep in my antechamber; but I did not think it worth while to put his valor to the proof.

With all the hardihood I had assumed and all the precautions I had taken, I must confess the first night passed in these quarters was inexpressibly dreary. I do not think it was so much the apprehension of dangers from without that affected me, as the character of the place itself, with all its strange associations: the deeds of violence committed there; the tragical ends of many of those who had once reigned there in splendor. As I passed beneath the fated halls of the Tower of Comares on the way to my chamber, I called to mind a quotation, that used to thrill me in the days of boyhood:

Fate sits on these dark battlements and frowns;

And, as the portal opens to receive me,

A voice in sullen echoes through the courts

Tells of a nameless deed!

The whole family escorted me to my chamber, and took leave of me as of one engaged on a perilous enterprise; and when I heard their retreating steps die away along the waste antechambers and echoing galleries; and turned the key of my door, I was reminded of those hobgoblin stories, where the hero is left to accomplish the adventure of an enchanted house.

Even the thoughts of the fair Elizabetta and the beauties of her court, who had once graced these chambers, now, by a perversion of fancy, added to the gloom. Here was the scene of their transient gayety and loveliness; here were the very traces of their elegance and enjoyment; but what and where were they? — Dust and ashes! tenants of the tomb! phantoms of the memory!

A vague and indescribable awe was creeping over me. I would fain have ascribed it to the thoughts of robbers awakened by the evening's conversation, but I felt it was something more unreal and absurd. The long-buried superstitions of the nursery were reviving, and asserting their power over my imagination. Every thing began to be affected by the working of my mind. The whispering of the wind, among the citron-trees beneath my window, had something sinister. I cast my eyes into the garden of Lindaraxa; the groves presented a gulf of shadows; the thickets, indistinct and ghastly shapes. I was glad to close the window, but my chamber itself became infected. There was a slight rustling noise overhead; a bat suddenly emerged from a broken panel of the ceiling, flitting about the room and athwart my solitary lamp; and as the fateful bird almost flouted my face with his noiseless wing, the grotesque faces carved in high relief in the cedar ceiling, whence he had emerged, seemed to mope and mow at me.

Rousing myself, and half smiling at this temporary weakness, I resolved to brave it out in the true spirit of the hero of the enchanted house; so, taking lamp in hand, I sallied forth to make a tour of the palace. Notwithstanding every mental exertion the task was a severe one. I had to traverse waste halls and mysterious galleries, where the rays of the lamp extended but a short distance around me. I walked, as it were, in a mere halo of light, walled in by impenetrable darkness. The vaulted corridors were as caverns; the ceilings of the halls were lost in gloom. I recalled all that had been said of the danger from interlopers in these remote and ruined apartments. Might not some vagrant foe be lurking before or behind me, in the outer darkness? My own shadow, cast upon the wall, began to disturb me. The echoes of my own footsteps along the corridors made me pause and look round. I was traversing scenes fraught with dismal recollections. One dark passage led down to the mosque where Yusef, the Moorish monarch, the finisher of the Alhambra, had been basely murdered. In another place, I trod the gallery where another monarch had been struck down by the poniard of a relative whom he had thwarted in his love.

A low murmuring sound, as of stifled voices and clanking chains, now reached me. It seemed to come from the Hall of the Abencerrages. I knew it to be the rush of water through subterranean channels, but it sounded strangely in the night, and reminded me of the dismal stories to which it had given rise.

Soon, however, my ear was assailed by sounds too fearfully real to be the work of fancy. As I was crossing the Hall of Ambassadors, low moans and broken ejaculations rose, as it were, from beneath my feet. I paused and listened. They then appeared to be outside of the tower — then again within. Then broke forth howlings as of an animal — then stifled shrieks and inarticulate ravings. Heard in that dead hour and singular place, the effect was thrilling. I had no desire for further perambulation; but returned to my chamber with infinitely more alacrity than I had sallied forth, and drew my breath more freely when once more within its walls and the door bolted behind me. When I awoke in the morning, with the sun shining in at my window and lighting up every part of the building with his cheerful and truth-telling beams, I could scarcely recall the shadows and fancies conjured up by the gloom of the preceding night; or believe that the scenes around me, so naked and apparent, could have been clothed with such imaginary horrors.

Still, the dismal howlings and ejaculations I had heard were not ideal; they were soon accounted for, however, by my handmaid Dolores: being the ravings of a poor maniac, a brother of her aunt, who was subject to violent paroxysms, during which he was confined in a vaulted room beneath the Hall of Ambassadors.

In the course of a few evenings a thorough change took place in the scene and its associations. The moon, which when I took possession of my new apartments was invisible, gradually gained each evening upon the darkness of the night, and at length rolled in full splendor above the towers, pouring a flood of tempered light into every court and hall. The garden beneath my window, before wrapped in gloom, was gently lighted up, the orange and citron trees were tipped with silver; the fountain sparkled in the moonbeams, and even the blush of the rose was faintly visible.

I now felt the poetic merit of the Arabic inscription on the walls: "How beauteous is this garden, where the flowers of the earth vie with the stars of the heaven! What can compare with the vase of yon alabaster fountain filled with crystal water? Nothing but the moon in her fulness, shining in the midst of an unclouded sky!"

On such heavenly nights I would sit for hours at my window inhaling the sweetness of the garden, and musing on the checkered fortunes of those whose history was dimly shadowed out in the elegant memorials around. Sometimes, when all was quiet, and the clock from the distant cathedral of Granada struck the midnight hour, I have sallied out on another tour and wandered over the whole building; but how different from my first tour! No longer dark and mysterious; no longer peopled with shadowy foes; no longer recalling scenes of violence and murder; all was open, spacious, beautiful; every thing called up pleasing and romantic fancies; Lindaraxa once more walked in her garden; the gay chivalry of Moslem Granada once more glittered about the Court of Lions! Who can do justice to a moonlight night in such a climate and such a place? The temperature of a summer midnight in Andalusia is perfectly ethereal. We seem lifted up into a purer atmosphere; we feel a serenity of soul, a buoyancy of spirits, an elasticity of frame, which render mere existence happiness. But when moonlight is added to all this, the effect is like enchantment. Under its plastic sway the Alhambra seems to regain its pristine glories. Every rent and chasm of time; every mouldering tint and weather-stain is gone; the marble resumes its original whiteness; the long colonnades brighten in the moonbeams; the halls are illuminated with a softened radiance — we tread the enchanted palace of an Arabian tale!

What a delight, at such a time, to ascend to the little airy pavilion of the queen's toilet (el tocador de la Reyna), which, like a bird-cage, overhangs the valley of the Darro, and gaze from its light arcades upon the moonlight prospect! To the right, the swelling mountains of the Sierra Nevada, robbed of their ruggedness and softened into a fairy land, with their snowy summits gleaming like silver clouds against the deep blue sky. And then to lean over the parapet of the Tocador and gaze down upon Granada and the Albaycin spread out like a map below; all buried in deep repose; the white palaces and convents sleeping in the moonshine, and beyond all these the vapory Vega fading away like a dream-land in the distance.

Sometimes the faint click of castanets rises from the Alameda, where some gay Andalusians are dancing away the summer night. Sometimes the dubious tones of a guitar and the notes of an amorous voice, tell perchance the whereabout of some moon-struck lover serenading his lady's window.

Such is a faint picture of the moonlight nights I have passed loitering about the courts and halls and balconies of this most suggestive pile, "feeding my fancy with sugared suppositions," and enjoying that mixture of reverie and sensation which steal away existence in a southern climate; so that it has been almost morning before I have retired to bed, and been lulled to sleep by the falling waters of the fountain of Lindaraxa.

Panorama from the Tower of Comares

It is a serene and beautiful morning: the sun has not gained sufficient power to destroy the freshness of the night. What a morning to mount to the summit of the Tower of Comares, and take a bird's-eye view of Granada and its environs!

Come then, worthy reader and comrade, follow my steps into this vestibule, ornamented with rich tracery, which opens into the Hall of Ambassadors. We will not enter the hall, however, but turn to this small door opening into the wall. Have a care! here are steep winding steps and but scanty light; yet up this narrow, obscure, and spiral staircase, the proud monarchs of Granada and their queens have often ascended to the battlements to watch the approach of invading armies, or gaze with anxious hearts on the battles in the Vega.

At length we have reached the terraced roof, and may take breath for a moment, while we cast a general eye over the splendid panorama of city and country; of rocky mountain, verdant valley, and fertile plain; of castle, cathedral, Moorish towers, and Gothic domes, crumbling ruins, and blooming groves. Let us approach the battlements, and cast our eyes immediately below. See, on this side we have the whole plain of the Alhambra laid open to us, and can look down into its courts and gardens. At the foot of the tower is the Court of the Alberca, with its great tank or fishpool, bordered with flowers; and yonder is the Court of Lions, with its famous fountain, and its light Moorish arcades; and in the centre of the pile is the little garden of Lindaraxa, buried in the heart of the building, with its roses and citrons, and shrubbery of emerald green.

That belt of battlements, studded with square towers straggling round the whole brow of the hill, is the outer boundary of the fortress. Some of the towers, you may perceive, are in ruins, and their massive fragments buried among vines, fig-trees and aloes.

Let us look on this northern side of the tower. It is a giddy height; the very foundations of the tower rise above the groves of the steep hill-side. And see I a long fissure in the massive walls, shows that the tower has been rent by some of the earthquakes, which from time to time have thrown Granada into consternation; and which, sooner or later, must reduce this crumbling pile to a mere mass of ruin. The deep narrow glen below us, which gradually widens as it opens from the mountains, is the valley of the Darro; you see the little river winding its way under imbowered terraces, and among orchards and flower-gardens. It is a stream famous in old times for yielding gold, and its sands are still sifted occasionally, in search of the precious ore. Some of those white pavilions, which here and there gleam from among groves and vineyards, were rustic retreats of the Moors, to enjoy the refreshment of their gardens. Well have they been compared by one of their poets to so many pearls set in a bed of emeralds.

The airy palace, with its tall white towers and long arcades, which breasts yon mountain, among pompous groves and hanging gardens, is the Generalife, a summer palace of the Moorish kings, to which they resorted during the sultry months to enjoy a still more breezy region than that of the Alhambra. The naked summit of the height above it, where you behold some shapeless ruins, is the Silla del Moro, or Seat of the Moor, so called from having been a retreat of the unfortunate Boabdil during the time of an insurrection, where he seated himself, and looked down mournfully upon his rebellious city.

A murmuring sound of water now and then rises from the valley. It is from the aqueduct of yon Moorish mill, nearly at the foot of the hill. The avenue of trees beyond is the Alameda, along the bank of the Darro, a favorite resort in evenings, and a rendezvous of lovers in the summer nights, when the guitar may be heard at a late hour from the benches along its walks. At present you see none but a few loitering monks there, and a group of water-carriers. The latter are burdened with water jars of ancient Oriental construction, such as were used by the Moors. They have been filled at the cold and limpid spring called the fountain of Avellanos. Yon mountain path leads to the fountain, a favorite resort of Moslems as well as Christians; for this is said to be the Adinamar (Aynu-l-adamar), the "Fountain of Tears," mentioned by Ibn Batuta the traveller, and celebrated in the histories and romances of the Moors.

You start! 'tis nothing but a hawk that we have frightened from his nest. This old tower is a complete breeding-place for vagrant birds; the swallow and martlet abound in every chink and cranny, and circle about it the whole day long; while at night, when all other birds have gone to rest, the moping owl comes out of its lurking-place, and utters its boding cry from the battlements. See how the hawk we have dislodged sweeps away below us, skimming over the tops of the trees, and sailing up to the ruins above the Generalife!

I see you raise your eyes to the snowy summit of yon pile of mountains, shining like a white summer cloud in the blue sky. It is the Sierra Nevada, the pride and delight of Granada; the source of her cooling breezes and perpetual verdure; of her gushing fountains and perennial streams. It is this glorious pile of mountains which gives to Granada that combination of delights so rare in a southern city: the fresh vegetation and temperate airs of a northern climate, with the vivifying ardor of a tropical sun, and the cloudless azure of a southern sky. It is this aerial treasury of snow, which, melting in proportion to the increase of the summer heat, sends down rivulets and streams through every glen and gorge of the Alpuxarras, diffusing emerald verdure and fertility throughout a chain of happy and sequestered valleys.

Those mountains may be well called the glory of Granada. They dominate the whole extent of Andalusia, and may be seen from its most distant parts. The muleteer hails them, as he views their frosty peaks from the sultry level of the plain; and the Spanish mariner on the deck of his bark, far, far off on the bosom of the blue Mediterranean, watches them with a pensive eye, thinks of delightful Granada, and chants, in low voice, some old romance about the Moors.

See to the south at the foot of those mountains a line of arid hills, down which a long train of mules is slowly moving. Here was the closing scene of Moslem domination. From the summit of one of those hills the unfortunate Boabdil cast back his last look upon Granada, and gave vent to the agony of his soul. It is the spot famous in song and story, "The last sigh of the Moor."

Further this way these arid hills slope down into the luxurious Vega, from which he had just emerged: a blooming wilderness of grove and garden, and teeming orchard, with the Xenil winding through it in silver links, and feeding innumerable rills; which, conducted through ancient Moorish channels, maintain the landscape in perpetual verdure. Here were the beloved bowers and gardens, and rural pavilions, for which the unfortunate Moors fought with such desperate valor. The very hovels and rude granges, now inhabited by boors, show, by the remains of arabesques and other tasteful decoration, that they were elegant residences in the days of the Moslems. Behold, in the very centre of this eventful plain, a place which in a manner links the history of the Old World with that of the New. Yon line of walls and towers gleaming in the morning sun, is the city of Santa Fe, built by the Catholic sovereigns during the siege of Granada, after a conflagration had destroyed their camp. It was to these walls Columbus was called back by the heroic queen, and within them the treaty was concluded which led to the discovery of the Western World. Behind yon promontory to the west is the bridge of Pinos, renowned for many a bloody fight between Moors and Christians. At this bridge the messenger overtook Columbus when, despairing of success with the Spanish sovereigns, he was departing to carry his project of discovery to the court of France.

Above the bridge a range of mountains bounds the Vega to the west: the ancient barrier between Granada and the Christian territories. Among their heights you may still discern warrior towns, their gray walls And battlements seeming of a piece with the rocks on which they are built. Here and there a solitary atalaya, or watchtower, perched on a mountain peak, looks down as it were from the sky into the valley on either side. How often have these atalayas given notice, by fire at night or smoke by day, of an approaching foe I It was down a cragged defile of these mountains, called the Pass of Lope, that the Christian armies descended into the Vega. Round the base of yon gray and naked mountain (the mountain of Elvira), stretching its bold rocky promontory into the bosom of the plain, the invading squadrons would come bursting into view, with flaunting banners and clangor of drum and trumpet.

Five hundred years have elapsed since Ismael ben Ferrag, a Moorish king of Granada, beheld from this very tower an invasion of the kind, and an insulting ravage of the Vega; on which occasion he displayed an instance of chivalrous magnanimity, often witnessed in the Moslem princes, "whose history," says an Arabian writer, "abounds in generous actions and noble deeds that will last through all succeeding ages, and live for ever in the memory of man."— But let us sit down on this parapet and I will relate the anecdote.

It was in the year of grace 1319, that Ismael ben Ferrag beheld from this tower a Christian camp whitening the skirts of yon mountain of Elvira. The royal princes, Don Juan and Don Pedro, regents of Castile during the minority of Alfonso XI, had already laid waste the country from Alcaudete to Alcala la Real, capturing the castle of Illora and setting fire to its suburbs, and they now carried their insulting ravages to the very gates of Granada, defying the king to sally forth and give them battle.

Ismael, though a young and intrepid prince, hesitated to accept the challenge. He had not sufficient force at hand, and awaited the arrival of troops summoned from the neighboring towns. The Christian princes, mistaking his motives, gave up all hope of drawing him forth, and having glutted themselves with ravage, struck their tents and began their homeward march. Don Pedro led the van, and Don Juan brought up the rear, but their march was confused and irregular, the army being greatly encumbered by the spoils and captives they had taken.

By this time King Ismael had received his expected resources, and putting them under the command of Osmyn, one of the bravest of his generals, sent them forth in hot pursuit of the enemy. The Christians were overtaken in the defiles of the mountains. A panic seized them; they were completely routed, and driven with great slaughter across the borders. Both of the princes lost their lives. The body of Don Pedro was carried off by his soldiers, but that of Don Juan was lost in the darkness of the night. His son wrote to the Moorish king, entreating that the body of his father might be sought and honorably treated. Ismael forgot in a moment that Don Juan was an enemy, who had carried ravage and insult to the very gate of his capital; he only thought of him as a gallant cavalier and a royal prince. By his command diligent search was made for the body. It was found in a barranco and brought to Granada. There Ismael caused it to be laid out in state on a lofty bier, surrounded by torches and tapers, in one of these halls of the Alhambra. Osmyn and other of the noblest cavaliers were appointed as a guard of honor, and the Christian captives were assembled to pray around it.

In the meantime, Ismael wrote to the son of Prince Juan to send a convoy for the body, assuring him it should be faithfully delivered up. In due time, a band of Christian cavaliers arrived for the purpose. They were honorably received and entertained by Ismael, and, on their departure with the body, the guard of honor of Moslem cavaliers escorted the funeral train to the frontier.

But enough — the sun is high above the mountains, and pours his full fervor on our heads. Already the terraced roof is hot beneath our feet; let us abandon it, and refresh ourselves under the Arcades by the Fountain of the Lions.

The Truant

We have had a scene of a petty tribulation in the Alhambra, which has thrown a cloud over the sunny countenance of Dolores. This little damsel has a female passion for pets of all kinds, and from the superabundant kindness of her disposition one of the ruined courts of the Alhambra is thronged with her favorites. A stately peacock and his hen seem to hold regal sway here, over pompous turkeys, querulous guinea-fowls, and a rabble rout of common cocks and hens. The great delight of Dolores, however has for some time past been centred in a youthful pair of pigeons, who have lately entered into the holy state of wedlock, and even supplanted a tortoise-shell cat and kittens in her affections.

As a tenement for them wherein to commence housekeeping, she had fitted up a small chamber adjacent to the kitchen, the window of which looked into one of the quiet Moorish courts. Here they lived in happy ignorance of any world beyond the court and its sunny roofs. Never had they aspired to soar above the battlements, or to mount to the summit of the towers. Their virtuous union was at length crowned by two spotless and milk-white eggs, to the great joy of their cherishing little mistress. Nothing could be more praiseworthy than the conduct of the young married folks on this interesting occasion. They took turns to sit upon the nest until the eggs were hatched, and while their callow progeny required warmth and shelter; while one thus stayed at home, the other foraged abroad for food, and brought home abundant supplies.

This scene of conjugal felicity has suddenly met with a reverse. Early this morning, as Dolores was feeding the male pigeon, she took a fancy to give him a peep at the great world. Opening a window, therefore, which looks down upon the valley of the Darro, she launched him at once beyond the walls of the Alhambra. For the first time in his life the astonished bird had to try the full vigor of his wings. He swept down into the valley, and then rising upwards with a surge, soared almost to the clouds. Never before had he risen to such a height, or experienced such delight in flying; and, like a young spendthrift just come to his estate, he seemed giddy with excess of liberty, and with the boundless field of action suddenly opened to him. For the whole day he has been circling about in capricious flights, from tower to tower, and tree to tree. Every attempt has been vain to lure him back by scattering grain upon the roofs; he seems to have lost all thought of home, of his tender helpmate, and his callow young. To add to the anxiety of Dolores, he has been joined by two palomas ladrones, or robber pigeons, whose instinct it is to entice wandering pigeons to their own dovecotes. The fugitive, like many other thoughtless youths on their first launching upon the world, seems quite fascinated with these knowing but graceless companions, who have undertaken to show him life, and introduce him to society. He has been soaring with them over all the roofs and steeples of Granada. A thunder-storm has passed over the city, but he has not sought his home; night has closed in, and still he comes not. To deepen the pathos of the affair, the female pigeon, after remaining several hours on the nest without being relieved, at length went forth to seek her recreant mate; but stayed away so long that the young ones perished for want of the warmth and shelter of the parent bosom. At a late hour in the evening, word was brought to Dolores, that the truant bird had been seen upon the towers of the Generalife. Now it happens that the Administrador of that ancient palace has likewise a dovecote, among the inmates of which are said to be two or three of these inveigling birds, the terror of all neighboring pigeon-fanciers. Dolores immediately concluded, that the two feathered sharpers who had been seen with her fugitive, were these bloods of the Generalife. A council of war was forthwith held in the chamber of Tia Antonia. The Generalife is a distinct jurisdiction from the Alhambra, and of course some punctilio, if not jealousy, exists between their custodians. It was determined, therefore, to send Pepe, the stuttering lad of the gardens, as ambassador to the Administrador, requesting that if such fugitive should be found in his dominions, he might be given up as a subject of the Alhambra. Pepe departed accordingly, on his diplomatic expedition, through the moonlit groves and avenues, but returned in an hour with the afflicting intelligence that no such bird was to be found in the dovecote of the Generalife. The Administrador, however, pledged his sovereign word that if such vagrant should appear there, even at midnight, he should instantly be arrested, and sent back prisoner to his little black-eyed mistress.

Thus stands the melancholy affair, which has occasioned much distress throughout the palace, and has sent the inconsolable Dolores to a sleepless pillow.

"Sorrow endureth for a night," says the proverb, "but joy cometh in the morning." The first object that met my eyes, on leaving my room this morning, was Dolores, with the truant pigeon in her hands, and her eyes sparkling with joy. He had appeared at an early hour on the battlements, hovering shyly about from roof to roof, but at length entered the window, and surrendered himself prisoner. He gained little credit, however, by his return; for the ravenous manner in which he devoured the food set before him showed that, like the prodigal son, he had been driven home by sheer famine. Dolores upbraided him for his faithless conduct, calling him all manner of vagrant names, though, woman-like, she fondled him at the same time to her bosom, and covered him with kisses. I observed, however, that she had taken care to clip his wings to prevent all future soarings; a precaution which I mention for the benefit of all those who have truant lovers or wandering husbands. More than one valuable moral might be drawn from the story of Dolores and her pigeon.

The Balcony

I have spoken of a balcony of the central window of the Hall of Ambassadors. It served as a kind of observatory, where I used often to take my seat, and consider not merely the heaven above but the earth beneath. Besides the magnificent prospect which it commanded of mountain, valley, and vega, there was a little busy scene of human life laid open to inspection immediately below. At the foot of the hill was an alameda, or public walk, which, though not so fashionable as the more modern and splendid paseo of the Xenil, still boasted a varied and picturesque concourse. Hither resorted the small gentry of the suburbs, together with priests and friars, who walked for appetite and digestion; majos and majas, the beaux and belles of the lower classes, in their Andalusian dresses; swaggering contrabandistas, and sometimes half-muffled and mysterious loungers of the higher ranks, on some secret assignation.

It was a moving picture of Spanish life and character, which I delighted to study; and as the astronomer has his grand telescope with which to sweep the skies, and, as it were, bring the stars nearer for his inspection, so I had a smaller one, of pocket size, for the use of my observatory, with which I could sweep the regions below, and bring the countenances of the motley groups so close as almost, at times, to make me think I could divine their conversation by the play and expression of their features. I was thus, in a manner, an invisible observer, and, without quitting my solitude, could throw myself in an instant into the midst of society — a rare advantage to one of somewhat shy and quiet habits, and fond, like myself, of observing the drama of life without becoming an actor in the scene.

There was a considerable suburb lying below the Alhambra, filling the narrow gorge of the valley, and extending up the opposite hill of the Albaycin. Many of the houses were built in the Moorish style, round patios, or courts, cooled by fountains and open to the sky; and as the inhabitants passed much of their time in these courts, and on the terraced roofs during the summer season, it follows that many a glance at their domestic life might be obtained by an aerial spectator like myself, who could look down on them from the clouds.

I enjoyed, in some degree, the advantages of the student in the famous old Spanish story, who beheld all Madrid unroofed for his inspection; and my gossiping squire, Mateo Ximenes, officiated occasionally as my Asmodeus, to give me anecdotes of the different mansions and their inhabitants.

I preferred, however, to form conjectural histories for myself, and thus would sit for hours, weaving, from casual incidents and indications passing under my eye, a whole tissue of schemes, intrigues, and occupations of the busy mortals below. There was scarce a pretty face or a striking figure that I daily saw, about which I had not thus gradually framed a dramatic story, though some of my characters would occasionally act in direct opposition to the part assigned them, and disconcert the whole drama. Reconnoitering one day with my glass the streets of the Albaycin, I beheld the procession of a novice about to take the veil; and remarked several circumstances which excited the strongest sympathy in the fate of the youthful being thus about to be consigned to a living tomb. I ascertained to my satisfaction that she was beautiful; and, from the paleness of her cheek, that she was a victim, rather than a votary. She was arrayed in bridal garments, and decked with a chaplet of white flowers, but her heart evidently revolted at this mockery of a spiritual union, and yearned after its earthly loves. A tall, stern-looking man walked near her in the procession; it was, of course, the tyrannical father, who, from some bigoted or sordid motive, had compelled this sacrifice. Amid the crowd was a dark handsome youth, in Andalusian garb, who seemed to fix on her an eye of agony. It was doubtless the secret lover from whom she was for ever to be separated. My indignation rose as I noted the malignant expression painted on the countenances of the attendant monks and friars. The procession arrived at the chapel of the convent; the sun gleamed for the last time upon the chaplet of the poor novice, as she crossed the fatal threshold, and disappeared within the building. The throng poured in with cowl, and cross, and minstrelsy; the lover paused for a moment at the door. I could divine the tumult of his feelings; but he mastered them, and entered. There was a long interval — I pictured to myself the scene passing within; the poor novice despoiled of her transient finery, and clothed in the conventual garb; the bridal chaplet taken from her brow, and her beautiful head shorn of its long silken tresses. I heard her murmur the irrevocable vow. I saw her extended on a bier: the death-pall spread over her, the funeral service performed that proclaimed her dead to the world; her sighs were drowned in the deep tones of the organ, and the plaintive requiem of the nuns; the father looked on, unmoved, without a tear; the lover — no — my imagination refused to portray the anguish of the lover — there the picture remained a blank.

After a time the throng again poured forth, and dispersed various ways, to enjoy the light of the sun and mingle with the stirring scenes of life; but the victim, with her bridal chaplet, was no longer there. The door of the convent closed that severed her from the world for ever. I saw the father and the lover issue forth; they were in earnest conversation. The latter was vehement in his gesticulations; I expected some violent termination to my drama; but an angle of a building interfered and closed the scene. My eye afterwards was frequently turned to that convent with painful interest. I remarked late at night a solitary light twinkling from a remote lattice of one of its towers. "There," said I, "the unhappy nun sits weeping in her cell, while perhaps her lover paces the street below in unavailing anguish."

The officious Mateo interrupted my meditations and destroyed in an instant the cobweb tissue of my fancy. With his usual zeal he had gathered facts concerning the scene, which put my fictions all to flight. The heroine of my romance was neither young nor handsome; she had no lover; she had entered the convent of her own free will, as a respectable asylum, and was one of the most cheerful residents within its walls.

It was some little while before I could forgive the wrong done me by the nun in being thus happy in her cell, in contradiction to all the rules of romance; I diverted my spleen, however, by watching, for a day or two, the pretty coquetries of a dark-eyed brunette, who, from the covert of a balcony shrouded with flowering shrubs and a silken awning, was carrying on a mysterious correspondence with a handsome, dark, well-whiskered cavalier, who lurked frequently in the street beneath her window. Sometimes I saw him at an early hour, stealing forth wrapped to the eyes in a mantle. Sometimes he loitered at a corner, in various disguises, apparently waiting for a private signal to slip into the house. Then there was the tinkling of a guitar at night, and a lantern shifted from place to place in the balcony. I imagined another intrigue like that of Almaviva; but was again disconcerted in all my suppositions. The supposed lover turned out to be the husband of the lady, and a noted contrabandista; and all his mysterious signs and movements had doubtless some smuggling scheme in view.

I occasionally amused myself with noting from this balcony the gradual changes of the scenes below, according to the different stages of the day.

Scarce has the gray dawn streaked the sky, and the earliest cock crowed from the cottages of the hill-side, when the suburbs give sign of reviving animation; for the fresh hours of dawning are precious in the summer season in a sultry climate. All are anxious to get the start of the sun, in the business of the day. The muleteer drives forth his loaded train for the journey; the traveller slings his carbine behind his saddle, and mounts his steed at the gate of the hostel; the brown peasant from the country urges forward his loitering beasts, laden with panniers of sunny fruit and fresh dewy vegetables: for already the thrifty housewives are hastening to the market. The sun is up and sparkles along the valley, tipping the transparent foliage of the groves. The matin bells resound melodiously through the pure bright air, announcing the hour of devotion. The muleteer halts his burdened animals before the chapel, thrusts his staff through his belt behind, and enters with hat in hand, smoothing his coal-black hair, to hear a mass, and put up a prayer for a prosperous wayfaring across the sierra. And now steals forth on fairy foot the gentle senora, in trim basquina, with restless fan in hand, and dark eye flashing from beneath the gracefully folded mantilla; she seeks some well-frequented church to offer up her morning orisons; but the nicely-adjusted dress, the dainty shoe and cobweb stocking, the raven tresses exquisitely braided, the fresh plucked rose, gleaming among them like a gem, show that earth divides with Heaven the empire of her thoughts. Keep an eye upon her, careful mother, or virgin aunt, or vigilant duenna, whichever you be, that walk behind I As the morning advances, the din of labor augments on every side; the streets are thronged with man, and steed, and beast of burden, and there is a hum and murmur, like the surges of the ocean. As the sun ascends to his meridian the hum and bustle gradually decline; at the height of noon there is a pause. The panting city sinks into lassitude, and for several hours there is a general repose. The windows are closed, the curtains drawn; the inhabitants retired into the coolest recesses of their mansions; the full-fed monk snores in his dormitory; the brawny porter lies stretched on the pavement beside his burden; the peasant and the laborer sleep beneath the trees of the Alameda, lulled by the sultry chirping of the locust. The streets are deserted, except by the water-carrier, who refreshes the ear by proclaiming the merits of his sparkling beverage, "colder than the mountain snow (mas fria que la nieve)."

As the sun declines, there is again a gradual reviving, and when the vesper bell rings out his sinking knell, all nature seems to rejoice that the tyrant of the day has fallen. Now begins the bustle of enjoyment, when the citizens pour forth to breathe the evening air, and revel away the brief twilight in the walks and gardens of the Darro and Xenil.

As night closes, the capricious scene assumes new features. Light after light gradually twinkles forth; here a taper from a balconied window; there a votive lamp before the image of a Saint. Thus, by degrees, the city emerges from the pervading gloom, and sparkles with scattered lights, like the starry firmament. Now break forth from court and garden, and street and lane, the tinkling of innumerable guitars, and the clicking of castanets; blending, at this lofty height, in a faint but general concert. "Enjoy the moment," is the creed of the gay and amorous Andalusian, and at no time does he practise it more zealously than in the balmy nights of summer, wooing his mistress with the dance, the love ditty, and the passionate serenade.

I was one evening seated in the balcony, enjoying the light breeze that came rustling along the side of the hill, among the tree-tops, when my humble historiographer Mateo, who was at my elbow, pointed out a spacious house, in an obscure street of the Albaycin, about which he related, as nearly as I can recollect, the following anecdote.

The Court of Lions

The peculiar charm of this dreamy old palace is its power of calling up vague reveries and picturings of the past, and thus clothing naked realities with the illusions of the memory and the imagination. As I delight to walk in these "vain shadows," I am prone to seek those parts of the Alhambra which are most favorable to this phantasmagoria of the mind; and none are more so than the Court of Lions, and its surrounding halls. Here the hand of time has fallen the lightest, and the traces of Moorish elegance and splendor exist in almost their original brilliancy. Earthquakes have shaken the foundations of this pile, and rent its rudest towers; yet see! not one of those slender columns has been displaced, not an arch of that light and fragile colonnade given way, and all the fairy fretwork of these domes, apparently as unsubstantial as the crystal fabrics of a morning's frost, exist after the lapse of centuries, almost as fresh as if from the hand of the Moslem artist. I write in the midst of these mementos of the past, in the fresh hour of early morning, in the fated Hall of the Abencerrages. The blood-stained fountain, the legendary monument of their massacre, is before me; the lofty jet almost casts its dew upon my paper. How difficult to reconcile the ancient tale of violence and blood with the gentle and peaceful scene around! Everything here appears calculated to inspire kind and happy feelings, for everything is delicate and beautiful. The very light falls tenderly from above, through the lantern of a dome tinted and wrought as if by fairy hands. Through the ample and fretted arch of the portal I behold the Court of Lions, with brilliant sunshine gleaming along its colonnades, and sparkling in its fountains. The lively swallow dives into the court and, rising with a surge, darts away twittering over the roofs; the busy bee toils humming among the flower beds, and painted butterflies hover from plant to plant, and flutter up and sport with each other in the sunny air. It needs but a slight exertion of the fancy to picture some pensive beauty of the harem, loitering in these secluded haunts of Oriental luxury.

He, however, who would behold this scene under an aspect more in unison with its fortunes, let him come when the shadows of evening temper the brightness of the court, and throw a gloom into surrounding halls. Then nothing can be more serenely melancholy, or more in harmony with the tale of departed grandeur.

At such times I am apt to seek the Hall of Justice, whose deep shadowy arcades extend across the upper end of the court. Here was performed, in presence of Ferdinand and Isabella, and their triumphant court, the pompous ceremonial of high mass, on taking possession of the Alhambra. The very cross is still to be seen upon the wall, where the altar was erected, and where officiated the Grand Cardinal of Spain, and others of the highest religious dignitaries of the land. I picture to myself the scene when this place was filled with the conquering host, that mixture of mitred prelate and shaven monk, and steel-clad knight and silken courtier; when crosses and crosiers and religious standards were mingled with proud armorial ensigns and the banners of haughty chiefs of Spain, and flaunted in triumph through these Moslem halls. I picture to myself Columbus, the future discoverer of a world, taking his modest stand in a remote corner, the humble and neglected spectator of the pageant. I see in imagination the Catholic sovereigns prostrating themselves before the altar, and pouring forth thanks for their victory; while the vaults resound with sacred minstrelsy, and the deep-toned Te Deum.

The transient illusion is over — the pageant melts from the fancy — monarch, priest, and warrior, return into oblivion, with the Moslems over whom they exulted. The hall of their triumph is waste and desolate. The bat flits about its twilight vault, and the owl hoots from the neighboring Tower of Comares.

Entering the Court of the Lions a few evenings since, I was almost startled at beholding a turbaned Moor quietly seated near the fountain. For a moment one of the fictions of the place seemed realized: an enchanted Moor had broken the spell of centuries, and become visible. He proved, however, to be a mere ordinary mortal; a native of Tetuan in Barbary, who had a shop in the Zacatin of Granada, where he sold rhubarb, trinkets, and perfumes. As he spoke Spanish fluently, I was enabled to hold conversation with him, and found him shrewd and intelligent. He told me that he came up the hill occasionally in the summer, to pass a part of the day in the Alhambra, which reminded him of the old palaces in Barbary, being built and adorned in similar style, though with more magnificence.

As we walked about the palace, he pointed out several of the Arabic inscriptions, as possessing much poetic beauty.

"Ah, senor," said he, "when the Moors held Granada, they were a gayer people than they are nowadays. They thought only of love, music, and poetry. They made stanzas upon every occasion, and set them all to music. He who could make the best verses, and she who had the most tuneful voice, might be sure of favor and preferment. In those days, if anyone asked for bread, the reply was, make me a couplet; and the poorest beggar, if he begged in rhyme, would often be rewarded with a piece of gold."

"And is the popular feeling for poetry," said I, "entirely lost among you?"

"By no means, senor; the people of Barbary, even those of lower classes, still make couplets, and good ones too, as in old times, but talent is not rewarded as it was then; the rich prefer the jingle of their gold to the sound of poetry or music."

As he was talking, his eye caught one of the inscriptions which foretold perpetuity to the power and glory of the Moslem monarchs, the masters of this pile. He shook his head, and shrugged his shoulders, as he interpreted it. "Such might have been the case," said he; "the Moslems might still have been reigning in the Alhambra, had not Boabdil been a traitor, and given up his capital to the Christians. The Spanish monarchs would never have been able to conquer it by open force."

I endeavored to vindicate the memory of the unlucky Boabdil from this aspersion, and to show that the dissensions which led to the downfall of the Moorish throne, originated in the cruelty of his tiger-hearted father; but the Moor would admit of no palliation.

"Muley Abul Hassan," said he, "might have been cruel; but he was brave, vigilant, and patriotic. Had he been properly seconded, Granada would still have been ours; but his son Boabdil thwarted his plans, crippled his power, sowed treason in his palace, and dissension in his camp. May the curse of God light upon him for his treachery!" With these words the Moor left the Alhambra.

71

The indignation of my turbaned companion agrees with an anecdote related by a friend, who, in the course of a tour in Barbary, had an interview with the Pacha of Tetuan. The Moorish governor was particular in his inquiries about Spain and especially concerning the favored region of Andalusia, the delights of Granada, and the remains of its royal palace. The replies awakened all those fond recollections, so deeply cherished by the Moors, of the power and splendor of their ancient empire in Spain. Turning to his Moslem attendants, the Pacha stroked his beard, and broke forth in passionate lamentations, that such a sceptre should have fallen from the sway of true believers. He consoled himself, however, with the persuasion, that the power and prosperity of the Spanish nation were on the decline; that a time would come when the Moors would reconquer their rightful domains; and that the day was perhaps not far distant, when Mohammedan worship would again be offered up in the Mosque of Cordova, and a Mohammedan prince sit on his throne in the Alhambra.

Such is the general aspiration and belief among the Moors of Barbary, who consider Spain, or Andaluz, as it was anciently called, their rightful heritage, of which they have been despoiled by treachery and violence. These ideas are fostered and perpetuated by the descendants of the exiled Moors of Granada, scattered among the cities of Barbary. Several of these reside in Tetuan, preserving their ancient names, such as Paez and Medina, and refraining from intermarriage with any families who cannot claim the same high origin. Their vaunted lineage is regarded with a degree of popular deference, rarely shown in Mohammedan communities to any hereditary distinction, excepting in the royal line.

These families, it is said, continue to sigh after the terrestrial paradise of their ancestors, and to put up prayers in their mosques on Fridays, imploring Allah to hasten the time when Granada shall be restored to the faithful: an event to which they look forward as fondly and confidently as did the Christian crusaders to the recovery of the Holy Sepulchre. Nay, it is added, that some of them retain the ancient maps and deeds of the estates and gardens of their ancestors at Granada, and even the keys of the houses, holding them as evidences of their hereditary claims, to be produced at the anticipated day of restoration.

My conversation with the Moor set me to musing on the fate of Boabdil. Never was surname more applicable than that bestowed upon him by his subjects of El Zogoybi, or the Unlucky. His misfortunes began almost in his cradle, and ceased not even with his death. If ever he cherished the desire of leaving an honorable name on the historic page, how cruelly has he been defrauded of his hopes! Who is there that has turned the least attention to the romantic history of the Moorish domination in Spain, without kindling with indignation at the alleged atrocities of Boabdil? Who has not been touched with the woes of his lovely and gentle queen, subjected by him to a trial of life and death, on a false charge of infidelity? Who has not been shocked by his alleged murder of his sister and her two children, in a transport of passion? Who has not felt his blood boil, at the inhuman massacre of the gallant Abencerrages, thirty-six of whom, it is affirmed, he ordered to be beheaded in the Court of Lions? All these charges have been reiterated in various forms; they have passed into ballads, dramas, and romances, until they have taken too thorough possession of the public mind to be eradicated. There is not a foreigner of education that visits the Alhambra but asks for the fountain where the Abencerrages were beheaded, and gazes with horror at the grated gallery where the queen is said to have been confined; not a peasant of the Vega or the Sierra, but sings the story in rude couplets, to the accompaniment of his guitar, while his hearers learn to execrate the very name of Boabdil.

Never, however, was name more foully and unjustly slandered. I have examined all the authentic chronicles and letters written by Spanish authors, contemporary with Boabdil, some of whom were in the confidence of the Catholic sovereigns, and actually present in the camp throughout the war. I have examined all the Arabian authorities I could get access to, through the medium of translation, and have found nothing to justify these dark and hateful accusations. The most of these tales may be traced to a work commonly called The Civil Wars of Granada, containing a pretended history of the feuds of the Zegries and Abencerrages, during the last struggle of the Moorish empire. The work appeared originally in Spanish, and professed to be translated from the Arabic by one Gines Perez de Hita, an inhabitant of Murcia. It has since passed into various languages, and Florian has taken from it much of the fable of his Gonsalvo of Cordova; it has thus, in a great measure, usurped the authority of real history, and is currently believed by the people, and especially the peasantry of Granada. The whole of it, however, is a mass of fiction, mingled with a few disfigured truths, which give it an air of veracity. It bears internal evidence of its falsity; the manners and customs of the Moors being extravagantly misrepresented in it, and scenes depicted totally incompatible with their habits and their faith, and which never could have been recorded by a Mahometan writer.

I confess there seems to me something almost criminal, in the wilful perversions of this work: great latitude is undoubtedly to be allowed to romantic fiction, but there are limits which it must not pass; and the names of the distinguished dead, which belong to history, are no more to be calumniated than those of the illustrious living. One would have thought, too, that the unfortunate Boabdil had suffered enough for his justifiable hostility to the Spaniards, by being stripped of his kingdom, without having his name thus wantonly traduced, and rendered a by-word and a theme of infamy in his native land, and in the very mansion of his fathers!

If the reader is sufficiently interested in these questions to tolerate a little historical detail, the following facts, gleaned from what appear to be authentic sources, and tracing the fortunes of the Abencerrages, may serve to exculpate the unfortunate Boabdil from the perfidious massacre of that illustrious line so shamelessly charged to him. It will also serve to throw a proper light upon the alleged accusation and imprisonment of his queen.

The Abencerrages

A grand line of distinction existed among the Moslems of Spain, between those of Oriental origin and those from Western Africa. Among the former the Arabs considered themselves the purest race, as being descended from the countrymen of the Prophet, who first raised the standard of Islam; among the latter, the most warlike and powerful were the Berber tribes from Mount Atlas and the deserts of Sahara, commonly known as Moors, who subdued the tribes of the sea-coast, founded the city of Morocco, and for a long time disputed with the oriental races the control of Moslem Spain.

Among the oriental races the Abencerrages held a distinguished rank, priding themselves on a pure Arab descent from the Beni Seraj, one of the tribes who were Ansares or Companions of the Prophet. The Abencerrages flourished for a time at Cordova; but probably repaired to Granada after the downfall of the Western Caliphat; it was there they attained their historical and romantic celebrity, being foremost among the splendid chivalry which graced the court of the Alhambra.

Their highest and most dangerous prosperity was during the precarious reign of Muhamed Nasar, surnamed El Hayzari, or the Left-handed. That ill-starred monarch, when he ascended the throne in 1423, lavished his favors upon this gallant line, making the head of the tribe, Yusef Aben Zeragh, his vizier, or prime minister, and advancing his relatives and friends to the most distinguished posts about the court. This gave great offence to other tribes, and caused intrigues among their chiefs. Muhamed lost popularity also by his manners. He was vain, inconsiderate, and haughty; disdained to mingle among his subjects; forbade those jousts and tournaments, the delight of high and low; and passed his time in the luxurious retirement of the Alhambra. The consequence was a popular insurrection; the palace was stormed; the king escaped through the gardens, fled to the sea-coast, crossed in disguise to Africa, and took refuge with his kinsman, the sovereign of Tunis.

Muhamed el Zaguer, cousin of the fugitive monarch, took possession of the vacant throne. He pursued a different course from his predecessor. He not only gave fetes and tourneys, but entered the lists himself, in grand and sumptuous array; he distinguished himself in managing his horse, in tilting, riding at the ring, and other chivalrous exercises; feasted with his cavaliers, and made them magnificent presents.

Those who had been in favor with his predecessor, now experienced a reverse; he manifested such hostility to them that more than five hundred of the principal cavaliers left the city. Yusef Aben Zeragh, with forty of the Abencerrages, abandoned Granada in the night, and sought the court of Juan the king of Castile. Moved by their representations, that young and generous monarch wrote letters to the sovereign of Tunis, inviting him to assist in punishing the usurper and restoring the exiled king to his throne. The faithful and indefatigable vizier accompanied the bearer of these letters to Tunis, where he rejoined his exiled sovereign. The letters were successful. Muhamed el Hayzari landed in Andalusia with five hundred African horse, and was joined by the Abencerrages and others of his adherents and by his Christian allies; wherever he appeared the people submitted to him; troops sent against him deserted to his standard; Granada was recovered without a blow; the usurper retreated to the Alhambra, but was beheaded by his own soldiers (1428), after reigning between two and three years.

El Hayzari, once more on the throne, heaped honors on the loyal vizier, through whose faithful services he had been restored, and once more the line of the Abencerrages basked in the sunshine of royal favor. El Hayzari sent ambassadors to King Juan, thanking him for his aid, and proposing a perpetual league of amity. The king of Castile required homage and yearly tribute. These the left-handed monarch refused, supposing the youthful king too, much engaged in civil war to enforce his claims. Again the kingdom of Granada was harassed by invasions, and its Vega laid waste. Various battles took place with various success. But El Hayzari's greatest danger was near at home. There was at that time in Granada a cavalier, Don Pedro Venegas by name, a Moslem by faith, but Christian by descent, whose early history borders on romance. He was of the noble house of Luque, but captured when a child, eight years of age, by Cid Yahia Alnayar, prince of Almeria, who adopted him as his son, educated him in the Moslem faith, and brought him up among his children, the Cetimerian princes, a proud family, descended in direct line from Aben Hud, one of the early Granadian kings. A mutual attachment sprang up between Don Pedro and the princess Cetimerien, a daughter of Cid Yahia, famous for her beauty, and whose name is perpetuated by the ruins of her palace in Granada; still bearing traces of Moorish elegance and luxury. In process of time they were married; and thus a scion of the Spanish house of Luque became engrafted on the royal stock of Aben Hud.

Such is the early story of Don Pedro Venegas, who at the time of which we treat was a man mature in years, and of an active, ambitious spirit. He appears to have been the soul of a conspiracy set on foot about this time, to topple Muhamed the Left-handed from his unsteady throne, and elevate in his place Yusef Aben Alhamar, the eldest of the Cetimerian princes. The aid of the king of Castile was to be secured, and Don Pedro proceeded on a secret embassy to Cordova for the purpose. He informed King Juan of the extent of the conspiracy; that Yusef Aben Alhamar could bring a large force to his standard as soon as he should appear in the Vega, and would acknowledge himself his vassal, if with his aid he should attain the crown. The aid was promised, and Don Pedro hastened back to Granada with the tidings. The conspirators now left the city, a few at a time, under various pretexts; and when King Juan passed the frontier, Yusef Aben Alhamar brought eight thousand men to his standard and kissed his hand in token of allegiance.

It is needless to recount the various battles by which the kingdom was desolated, and the various intrigues by which one half of it was roused to rebellion. The Abencerrages stood by the failing fortunes of Muhamed throughout the struggle; their last stand was at Loxa, where their chief, the vizier Yusef Aben Zeragh, fell bravely fighting, and many of their noblest cavaliers were slain: in fact, in that disastrous war the fortunes of the family were nearly wrecked.

Again, the ill-starred Muhamed was driven from his throne, and took refuge in Malaga, the alcayde of which still remained true to him.

Yusef Aben Alhamar, commonly known as Yusef II, entered Granada in triumph on the first of January, 1432, but he found it a melancholy city, where half of the inhabitants were in mourning. Not a noble family but had lost some member; and in the slaughter of the Abencerrages at Loxa, had fallen some of the brightest of the chivalry.

The royal pageant passed through silent streets, and the barren homage of a court in the halls of the Alhambra ill supplied the want of sincere and popular devotion. Yusef Aben Alhamar felt the insecurity of his position. The deposed monarch was at hand in Malaga; the sovereign of Tunis espoused his cause, and pleaded with the Christian monarchs in his favor; above all, Yusef felt his own unpopularity in Granada; previous fatigues had impaired his health, a profound melancholy settled upon him, and in the course of six months he sank into the grave.

At the news of his death, Muhamed the Left-handed hastened from Malaga, and again was placed on the throne. From the wrecks of the Abencerrages he chose as viziers Abdelbar, one of the worthiest of that magnanimous line. Through his advice he restrained his vindictive feelings and adopted a conciliatory policy. He pardoned most of his enemies. Yusef, the defunct usurper, had left three children. His estates were apportioned among them. Aben Celim, the oldest son, was confirmed in the title of Prince of Almeria and Lord of Marchena in the Alpuxarras. Ahmed, the youngest, was made Senor of Luchar; and Equivila, the daughter, received rich patrimonial lands in the fertile Vega, and various houses and shops in the Zacatin of Granada. The vizier Abdelbar counselled the king, moreover, to secure the adherence of the family by matrimonial connections. An aunt of Muhamed was accordingly given in marriage to Aben Celim, while the prince Nasar, younger brother of the deceased usurper, received the hand of the beautiful Lindaraxa, daughter of Muhamed's faithful adherent, the alcayde of Malaga. This was the Lindaraxa whose name still designates one of the gardens of the Alhambra.

Don Pedro de Venegas alone, the husband of the princess Cetimerien, received no favor. He was considered as having produced the late troubles by his intrigues. The Abencerrages charged him with the reverses of their family and the deaths of so many of their bravest cavaliers. The king never spoke of him but by the opprobrious appellation of the Tornadizo, or Renegade. Finding himself in danger of arrest and punishment, he took leave of his wife, the princess, his two sons, Abul Cacim and Reduan, and his daughter, Cetimerien, and fled to Jaen. There, like his brother-in-law, the usurper, he expiated his intrigues and irregular ambition by profound humiliation and melancholy, and died in 1434 a penitent, because a disappointed man.

Muhamed el Hayzari was doomed to further reverses. He had two nephews, Aben Osmyn, surnamed El Anaf, or the Lame, and Aben Ismael. The former, who was of an ambitious spirit, resided in Almeria; the latter in Granada, where he had many friends. He was on the point of espousing a beautiful girl, when his royal uncle interfered and gave her to one of his favorites. Enraged at this despotic act, the prince Aben Ismael took horse and weapons and sallied from Granada for the frontier, followed by numerous cavaliers. The affair gave general disgust, especially to the Abencerrages who were attached to the prince. No sooner did tidings reach

Aben Osmyn of the public discontent than his ambition was aroused. Throwing himself suddenly into Granada, he raised a popular tumult, surprised his uncle in the Alhambra, compelled him to abdicate, and proclaimed himself king. This occurred in September, 1445.

The Abencerrages now gave up the fortunes of the left-handed king as hopeless, and himself as incompetent to rule. Led by their kinsman, the vizier Abdelbar, and accompanied by many other cavaliers, they abandoned the court and took post in Montefrio. Thence Abdelbar wrote to Prince Aben Ismael, who had taken refuge in Castile, inviting him to the camp, offering to support his pretensions to the throne, and advising him to leave Castile secretly, lest his departure should be opposed by King Juan II. The prince, however, confiding in the generosity of the Castilian monarch, told him frankly the whole matter. He was not mistaken. King Juan not merely gave him permission to depart, but promised him aid, and gave him letters to that effect to his commanders on the frontiers. Aben Ismael departed with a brilliant escort, arrived in safety at Montefrio, and was proclaimed king of Granada by Abdelbar and his partisans, the most important of whom were the Abencerrages. A long course of civil wars ensued between the two cousins, rivals for the throne. Aben Osmyn was aided by the kings of Navarre and Aragon, while Juan II, at war with his rebellious subjects, could give little assistance to Aben Ismael.

Thus for several years the country was torn by internal strife and desolated by foreign inroads, so that scarce a field but was stained with blood. Aben Osmyn was brave, and often signalized himself in arms; but he was cruel and despotic, and ruled with an iron hand. He offended the nobles by his caprices, and the populace by his tyranny, while his rival cousin conciliated all hearts by his benignity. Hence there were continual desertions from Granada to the fortified camp at Montefrio, and the party of Aben Ismael was constantly gaining strength. At length the king of Castile, having made peace with the kings of Aragon and Navarre, was enabled to send a choice body of troops to the assistance of Aben Ismael. The latter now left his trenches in Montefrio, and took the field. The combined forces marched upon Granada. Aben Osmyn sallied forth to the encounter. A bloody battle ensued, in which both of the rival cousins fought with heroic valor. Aben Osmyn was defeated and driven back to his gates. He summoned the inhabitants to arms, but few answered to his call; his cruelty had alienated all hearts. Seeing his fortunes at an end, he determined to close his career by a signal act of vengeance. Shutting himself up in the Alhambra, he summoned thither a number of the principal cavaliers whom he suspected of disloyalty. As they entered, they were one by one put to death. This is supposed by some to be the massacre which gave its fatal name to the Hall of the Abencerrages. Having perpetrated this atrocious act of vengeance, and hearing by the shouts of the populace that Aben Ismael was already proclaimed king in the city, he escaped with his satellites by the Cerro del Sol and the valley of the Darro to the Alpuxarra mountains, where he and his followers led a kind of robber life, laying villages and roads under contribution.

Aben Ismael II, who thus attained the throne in 1454, secured the friendship of King Juan II by acts of homage and magnificent presents. He gave liberal rewards to those who had been faithful to him, and consoled the families of those who had fallen in his cause. During his reign, the Abencerrages were again among the most favored of the brilliant chivalry that graced his court. Aben Ismael, however, was not of a warlike spirit; his reign was distinguished rather by works of public utility, the ruins of some of which are still to be seen on the Cerro del Sol.

In the same year of 1454 Juan II died, and was succeeded by Henry IV of Castile, surnamed the Impotent. Aben Ismael neglected to renew the league of amity with him which had existed with his predecessor, as he found it to be unpopular with the people of Granada. King Henry resented the omission, and, under pretext of arrears of tribute, made repeated forays into the kingdom of Granada. He gave countenance also to Aben Osmyn and his robber hordes, and took some of them into pay; but his proud cavaliers refused to associate with infidel outlaws, and determined to seize Aben Osmyn; who, however, made his escape, first to Seville, and thence to Castile.

In the year 1456, on the occasion of a great foray into the Vega by the Christians, Aben Ismael, to secure a peace, agreed to pay the king of Castile a certain tribute annually, and at the same time to liberate six hundred Christian captives; or, should the number of captives fall short, to make it up in Moorish hostages. Aben Ismael fulfilled the rigorous terms of the treaty, and reigned for a number of years with more tranquillity than usually fell to the lot of the monarchs of that belligerent kingdom. Granada enjoyed a great state of prosperity during his reign, and was the seat of festivity and splendor. His sultana was a daughter of Cid Hiaya Abraham Alnayar, prince of Almeria; and he had by her two sons, Abul Hassan, and Abi Abdallah, surnamed El Zagal, the father and uncle of Boabdil. We approach now the eventful period signalized by the conquest of Granada.

Muley Abul Hassan succeeded to the throne on the death of his father in 1465. One of his first acts was to refuse payment of the degrading tribute exacted by the Castilian monarch. His refusal was one of the causes of the subsequent disastrous war. I confine myself, however, to facts connected with the fortunes of the Abencerrages and the charges advanced against Boabdil.

The reader will recollect that Don Pedro Venegas, surnamed El Tornadizo, when he fled from Granada in 1433, left behind him two sons, Abul Cacim and Reduan, and a daughter, Cetimerien. They always enjoyed a distinguished rank in Granada, from their royal descent by the mother's side; and from being connected, through the princes of Almeria, with the last and the present king. The sons had distinguished themselves by their talents and bravery, and the daughter Cetimerien was married to Cid Hiaya, grandson of King Yusef and brother-in-law of El Zagal. Thus powerfully connected, it is not surprising to find Abul Cacim Venegas advanced to the post of vizier of Muley Abul Hassan, and Reduan Venegas one of his most favored generals. Their rise was regarded with an evil eye by the Abencerrages, who remembered the disasters brought upon their family, and the deaths of so many of their line, in the war fomented by the intrigues of Don Pedro, in the days of Yusef Aben Alhamar. A feud had existed ever since between the Abencerrages and the house of Venegas. It was soon to be aggravated by a formidable schism which took place in the royal harem.

Muley Abul Hassan, in his youthful days, had married his cousin, the princess Ayxa la Horra, daughter of his uncle, the ill-starred sultan, Muhamed the Left-handed; by her he had two sons, the eldest of whom was Boabdil, heir presumptive to the throne. Unfortunately at an advanced age he took another wife, Isabella de Solis, a young and beautiful Christian captive; better known by her Moorish appellation of Zoraya; by her he had also two sons. Two factions were produced in the palace by the rivalry of the sultanas, who were each anxious to secure for their children the succession to the throne. Zoraya was supported by the vizier Abul Cacim Venegas, his brother Reduan Venegas, and their numerous connections, partly through sympathy with her as being, like themselves, of Christian lineage, and partly because they saw she was the favorite of the doting monarch.

The Abencerrages, on the contrary, rallied round the sultana Ayxa; partly through hereditary opposition to the family of Venegas, but chiefly, no doubt, through a strong feeling of loyalty to her as daughter of Muhamed Alhayzari, the ancient benefactor of their line.

The dissensions of the palace went on increasing. Intrigues of all kinds took place, as is usual in royal palaces. Suspicions were artfully instilled in the mind of Muley Abul Hassan that Ayxa was engaged in a plot to depose him and put her son Boabdil on the throne. In his first transports of rage he confined them both in the Tower of Comares, threatening the life of Boabdil. At dead of night the anxious mother lowered her son from a window of the tower by the scarfs of herself and her female attendants; and some of her adherents, who were in waiting with swift horses, bore him away to the Alpuxarras. It is this imprisonment of the sultana Ayxa which possibly gave rise to the fable of the queen of Boabdil being confined by him in a tower to be tried for her life. No other shadow of a ground exists for it, and here we find the tyrant jailer was his father, and the captive sultana, his mother.

The massacre of the Abencerrages in the halls of the Alhambra, is placed by some about this time, and attributed also to Muley Abul Hassan, on suspicion of their being concerned in the conspiracy. The sacrifice of a number of the cavaliers of that line is said to have been suggested by the vizier Abul Cacim Venegas, as a means of striking terror into the rest. If such were really the case, the barbarous measure proved abortive. The Abencerrages continued intrepid, as they were loyal, in their adherence to the cause of Ayxa and her son Boabdil, throughout the war which ensued, while the Venegas were ever foremost in the ranks of Muley Abul Hassan and El Zagal. The ultimate fortunes of these rival families is worthy of note. The Venegas, in the last struggle of Granada, were among those who submitted to the conquerors, renounced the Moslem creed, returned to the faith from which their ancestor had apostatized, were rewarded with offices and estates, intermarried with Spanish families, and have left posterity among the nobles of the land. The Abencerrages remained true to their faith, true to their king, true to their desperate cause, and went down with the foundering wreck of Moslem domination, leaving nothing behind them but a gallant and romantic name in history.

In this historical outline, I trust I have shown enough to put the fable concerning Boabdil and the Abencerrages in a true light. The story of the accusation of his queen, and his cruelty to his sister, are equally void of foundation. In his domestic relations he appears to have been kind and affectionate. History gives him but one wife, Morayma, the daughter of the veteran alcayde of Loxa, old Aliatar, famous in song and story for his exploits in border warfare; and who fell in that disastrous foray into the Christian lands in which Boabdil was taken prisoner. Morayma was true to Boabdil throughout all his vicissitudes. When he was dethroned by the Castilian monarchs, she retired with him to the petty domain allotted him in the valleys of the Alpuxarras. It was only when (dispossessed of this by the jealous precautions and subtle chicanery of Ferdinand, and elbowed, as it were, out of his native land) he was preparing to embark for Africa, that her health and spirits, exhausted by anxiety and long suffering, gave way, and she fell into a lingering illness, aggravated by corroding melancholy. Boabdil was constant and affectionate to her to the last; the sailing of the ships was delayed for several weeks, to the great annoyance of the suspicious Ferdinand. At length Morayma sank into the grave, evidently the victim of a broken heart, and the event was reported to Ferdinand by his agent, as one propitious to his purposes, removing the only obstacle to the embarkation of Boabdil.

Mementos of Boabdil

While my mind was still warm with the subject of the unfortunate Boabdil, I set forth to trace the mementos of him still existing in this scene of his sovereignty and misfortunes. In the Tower of Comares, immediately under the Hall of Ambassadors, are two vaulted rooms, separated by a narrow passage; these are said to have been the prisons of himself and his mother, the virtuous Ayxa la Horra; indeed, no other part of the tower would have served for the purpose. The external walls of these chambers are of prodigious thickness, pierced with small windows secured by iron bars. A narrow stone gallery, with a low parapet, extends along three sides of the tower just below the windows, but at a considerable height from the ground. From this gallery, it is presumed, the queen lowered her son with the scarfs of herself and her female attendants during the darkness of the night to the hillside, where some of his faithful adherents waited with fleet steeds to bear him to the mountains.

Between three and four hundred years have elapsed, yet this scene of the drama remains almost unchanged. As I paced the gallery, my imagination pictured the anxious queen leaning over the parapet; listening, with the throbbings of a mother's heart, to the last echoes of the horses' hoofs as her son scoured along the narrow valley of the Darro.

I next sought the gate by which Boabdil made his last exit from the Alhambra, when about to surrender his capital and kingdom. With the melancholy caprice of a broken spirit, or perhaps with some superstitious feeling, he requested of the Catholic monarchs that no one afterwards might be permitted to pass through it. His prayer, according to ancient chronicles, was complied with, through the sympathy of isabella, and the gate was walled up.*

*Ay una puerta en la Alhambra por la qual salio Chico Rey de los Moros, quando si rindio prisionero al Rey de Espana D. Fernando, y le entrego la ciudad con el castillo. Pidio esta principe como por merced, y en memoria de tan importante conquista, al que quedasse siempre cerrada esta puerta. Consintio en allo el Rey Fernando, y des de aquel tiempo no solamente no se abrio la puerta sino tambien se construyo junto a ella fuerte bastion. — MORERI'S Historical Dictionary.

[There was a gate in the Alhambra by which Chico the King of the Moors went out when he gave himself up as a prisoner to the King of Spain, Don Ferdinand, and surrendered to him the city and the castle. This prince asked as a favor, and in memory of such an important conquest, that this portal always remain closed. King Ferdinand consented to this, and from that time not only was the gate not opened but also a strong bastion was constructed around it.]

I inquired for some time in vain for such a portal; at length my humble attendant, Mateo Ximenes, said it must be one closed up with stones, which, according to what he had heard from his father and grandfather, was the gateway by which King Chico had left the fortress. There was a mystery about it, and it had never been opened within the memory of the oldest inhabitant.

He conducted me to the spot. The gateway is in the centre of what was once an immense pile, called the Tower of the Seven Floors (la Torre de los Siete Suelos). It is famous in the neighborhood as the scene of strange apparitions and Moorish enchantments. According to Swinburne the traveller, it was originally the great gate of entrance. The antiquaries of Granada pronounce it the entrance to that quarter of the royal residence where the king's bodyguards were stationed. It therefore might well form an immediate entrance and exit to the palace; while the grand Gate of Justice served as the entrance of state to the fortress. When Boabdil sallied by this gate to descend to the Vega, where he was to surrender the keys of the city to the Spanish sovereigns, he left his vizier Aben Comixa to receive, at the Gate of Justice, the detachment from the Christian army and the officers to whom the fortress was to be given up.*

*The minor details of the surrender of Granada have been stated in different ways even by eye-witnesses. The author, in his revised edition of the Conquest, has endeavored to adjust them according to the latest and apparently best authorities.

The once redoubtable Tower of the Seven Floors is now a mere wreck, having been blown up with gunpowder by the French, when they abandoned the fortress. Great masses of the wall lie scattered about, buried in luxuriant herbage, or overshadowed by vines and fig-trees. The arch of the gateway, though rent by the shock, still remains; but the last wish of poor Boabdil has again, though unintentionally, been fulfilled, for the portal has been closed up by loose stones gathered from the ruins, and remains impassable.

Mounting my horse, I followed up the route of the Moslem monarch from this place of his exit. Crossing the hill of Los Martyros, and keeping along the garden wall of a convent bearing the same name, I descended a rugged ravine beset by thickets of aloes and Indian figs, and lined with caves and hovels swarming with gipsies. The descent was so steep and broken that I was fain to alight and lead my horse. By this via dolorosa poor Boabdil took his sad departure to avoid passing through the city; partly, perhaps, through unwillingness that its inhabitants should behold his humiliation; but chiefly, in all probability, lest it might cause some popular agitation. For the last reason, undoubtedly, the detachment sent to take possession of the fortress ascended by the same route.

Emerging from this rough ravine, so full of melancholy associations, and passing by the puerta de los molinos (the gate of the mills), I issued forth upon the public promenade called the Prado, and pursuing the course of the Xenil, arrived at a small chapel, once a mosque, now the Hermitage of San Sebastian. Here, according to tradition, Boabdil surrendered the keys of Granada to King Ferdinand. I rode slowly thence across the Vega to a village where the family and household of the unhappy king awaited him, for he had sent them forward on the preceding night from the Alhambra, that his mother and wife might not participate in his personal humiliation, or be exposed to the gaze of the conquerors. Following on in the route of the melancholy band of royal exiles, I arrived at the foot of a chain of barren and dreary heights, forming the skirt of the Alpuxarra mountains. From the summit of one of these the unfortunate Boabdil took his last look at Granada; it bears a name expressive of his sorrows, la Cuesta de las Lagrimas (the Hill of Tears). Beyond it, a sandy road winds across a rugged cheerless waste, doubly dismal to the unhappy monarch, as it led to exile.

I spurred my horse to the summit of a rock, where Boabdil uttered his last sorrowful exclamation, as he turned his eyes from taking their farewell gaze; it is still denominated el ultimo suspiro del Moro (the last sigh of the Moor). Who can wonder at his anguish at being expelled from such a kingdom and such an abode? With the Alhambra he seemed to be yielding up all the honors of his line, and all the glories and delights of life.

It was here, too, that his affliction was embittered by the reproach of his mother, Ayxa, who had so often assisted him in times of peril, and had vainly sought to instil into him her own resolute spirit. "You do well," said she, "to weep as a woman over what you could not defend as a man"; a speech savoring more of the pride of the princess than the tenderness of the mother.

When this anecdote was related to Charles V by Bishop Guevara, the emperor joined in the expression of scorn at the weakness of the wavering Boabdil. "Had I been he, or he been I," said the haughty potentate, "I would rather have made this Alhambra my sepulchre than have lived without a kingdom in the Alpuxarra." How easy it is for those in power and prosperity to preach heroism to the vanquished! how little can they understand that life itself may rise in value with the unfortunate, when nought but life remains I

Slowly descending the "Hill of Tears," I let my horse take his own loitering gait back to Granada, while I turned the story of the unfortunate Boabdil over in my mind. In summing up the particulars I found the balance inclining in his favor. Throughout the whole of his brief, turbulent, and disastrous reign, he gives evidence of a mild and amiable character. He, in the first instance, won the hearts of his people by his affable and gracious manners; he was always placable, and never inflicted any severity of punishment upon those who occasionally rebelled against him. He was personally brave; but wanted moral courage; and, in times of difficulty and perplexity, was wavering and irresolute. This feebleness of spirit hastened his downfall, while it deprived him of that heroic grace which would have given grandeur and dignity to his fate, and rendered him worthy of closing the splendid drama of the Moslem domination in Spain.

Public Fetes of Granada

My devoted squire and whilom ragged cicerone Mateo Ximenes, had a poor-devil passion for fates and holidays, and was never so eloquent as when detailing the civil and religious festivals of Granada. During the preparations for the annual Catholic fete of Corpus Christi, he was in a state of incessant transition between the Alhambra and the subjacent city, bringing me daily accounts of the magnificent arrangements that were in progress, and endeavoring, but in vain, to lure me down from my cool and airy retreat to witness them. At length, on the eve of the eventful day I yielded to his solicitations and descended from the regal halls of the Alhambra under his escort, as did of yore the adventure-seeking Haroun Alraschid, under that of his Grand Vizier Giaffar. Though it was yet scarce sunset, the city gates were already thronged with the picturesque villagers of the mountains, and the brown peasantry of the Vega. Granada has ever been the rallying place of a great mountainous region, studded with towns and villages. Hither, during the Moorish domination, the chivalry of this region repaired, to join in the splendid and semi-warlike fetes of the Vivarrambla, and hither the elite of its population still resort to join in the pompous ceremonials of the church. Indeed, many of the mountaineers from the Alpuxarras and the Sierra de Ronda, who now bow to the cross as zealous Catholics, bear the stamp of their Moorish origin, and are indubitable descendants of the fickle subjects of Boabdil.

Under the guidance of Mateo, I made my way through streets already teeming with a holiday population, to the square of the Vivarrambla, that great place for tilts and tourneys, so often sung in the Moorish ballads of love and chivalry. A gallery or arcade of wood had been erected along the sides of the square, for the grand religious procession of the following day. This was brilliantly illuminated for the evening as a promenade; and bands of music were stationed on balconies on each of the four facades of the square. All the fashion and beauty of Granada, all of its population of either sex that had good looks or fine clothes to display, thronged this arcade, promenading round and round the Vivarrambla. Here, too, were the majos and majas, the rural beaux and belles, with fine forms, flashing eyes, and gay Andalusian costumes; some of them from Ronda itself, that strong-hold of the mountains, famous for contrabandistas, bull-fighters, and beautiful women.

While this gay but motley throng kept up a constant circulation in the gallery, the centre of the square was occupied by the peasantry from the surrounding country; who made no pretensions to display, but came for simple, hearty enjoyment. The whole square was covered with them; forming separate groups of families and neighborhoods, like gipsy encampments, some were listening to the traditional ballad drawled out to the tinkling of the guitar, some were engaged in gay conversation, some were dancing to the click of the castanet. As I threaded my way through this teeming region with Mateo at my heels, I passed occasionally some rustic party, seated on the ground, making a merry though frugal repast. If they caught my eye as I loitered by, they almost invariably invited me to partake of their simple fare. This hospitable usage, inherited from their Moslem invaders, and originating in the tent of the Arab, is universal throughout the land, and observed by the poorest Spaniard.

As the night advanced, the gayety gradually died away in the arcades; the bands of music ceased to play, and the brilliant crowd dispersed to their homes. The centre of the square still remained well peopled, and Mateo assured me that the greater part of the peasantry, men, women, and children, would pass the night there, sleeping on the bare earth beneath the open canopy of heaven. Indeed, a summer night requires no shelter in this favored climate; and a bed is a superfluity, which many of the hardy peasantry of Spain never enjoy, and which some of them affect to despise. The common Spaniard wraps himself in his brown cloak, stretches himself on his manta or mule-cloth, and sleeps soundly, luxuriously accommodated if he can have a saddle for a pillow. In a little while the words of Mateo were made good; the peasant multitude nestled down on the ground to their night's repose, and by midnight, the scene on the Vivarrambla resembled the bivouac of an army.

The next morning, accompanied by Mateo, I revisited the square at sunrise. It was still strewed with groups of sleepers: some were reposing from the dance and revel of the evening; others, who had left their villages after work on the preceding day, having trudged on foot the greater part of the night, were taking a sound sleep to freshen themselves for the festivities of the day. Numbers from the mountains, and the remote villages of the plain, who had set out in the night, continued to arrive with their wives and children. All were in high spirits; greeting each other and exchanging jokes and pleasantries. The gay tumult thickened as the day advanced. Now came pouring in at the city gates, and parading through the streets, the deputations from the various villages, destined to swell the grand procession. These village deputations were headed by their priests, bearing their respective crosses and banners, and images of the blessed Virgin and of patron saints; all which were matters of great rivalship and jealousy among the peasantry. It was like the chivalrous gatherings of ancient days, when each town and village sent its chiefs, and warriors, and standards, to defend the capital, or grace its festivities.

At length all these various detachments congregated into one grand pageant, which slowly paraded round the Vivarrambla, and through the principal streets, where every window and balcony was hung with tapestry. In this procession were all the religious orders, the civil and military authorities, and the chief people of the parishes and villages: every church and convent had contributed its banners, its images, its relics, and poured forth its wealth for the occasion. In the centre of the procession walked the archbishop, under a damask canopy, and surrounded by inferior dignitaries and their dependants. The whole moved to the swell and cadence of numerous bands of music, and, passing through the midst of a countless yet silent multitude, proceeded onward to the cathedral.

I could not but be struck with the changes of times and customs, as I saw this monkish pageant passing through the Vivarrambla, the ancient seat of Moslem pomp and chivalry. The contrast was indeed forced upon the mind by the decorations of the square. The whole front of the wooden gallery erected for the procession, extending several hundred feet, was faced with canvas, on which some humble though patriotic artist had painted, by contract, a series of the principal scenes and exploits of the Conquest, as recorded in chronicle and romance. It is thus the romantic legends of Granada mingle themselves with every thing, and are kept fresh in the public mind.

As we wended our way back to the Alhambra, Mateo was in high glee and garrulous vein. "Ah, senor," exclaimed he, "there is no place in all the world like Granada for grand ceremonies (funciones grandes); a man need spend nothing on pleasure here, it is all furnished him gratis. Pero, el dia de la Toma! ah, senor! el dia de la Toma!" "But the day of the Taking! ah, senor, the day of the Taking"— that was the great day which crowned Mateo's notions of perfect felicity. The Dia de la Toma, I found, was the anniversary of the capture or taking possession of Granada, by the army of Ferdinand and Isabella.

On that day, according to Mateo, the whole city is abandoned to revelry. The great alarm bell on the watchtower of the Alhambra (la Torre de la vela), sends forth its clanging peals from morn till night; the sound pervades the whole Vega, and echoes along the mountains, summoning the peasantry from far and near to the festivities of the metropolis. "Happy the damsel," says Mateo, "who can get a chance to ring that bell; it is a charm to insure a husband within the year."

Throughout the day the Alhambra is thrown open to the public. Its halls and courts, where the Moorish monarchs once held sway, resound with the guitar and castanet, and gay groups, in the fanciful dresses of Andalusia, perform their traditional dances inherited from the Moors.

A grand procession, emblematic of the taking possession of the city, moves through the principal streets. The banner of Ferdinand and Isabella, that previous relic of the Conquest, is brought forth from its depository, and borne in triumph by the Alferez mayor, or grand standard-bearer. The portable camp-altar, carried about with the sovereigns in all their campaigns, is transported into the chapel royal of the cathedral, and placed before their sepulchre, where their effigies lie in monumental marble. High mass is then performed in memory of the Conquest; and at a certain part of the ceremony the Alferez mayor puts on his hat, and waves the standard above the tomb of the conquerors.

A more whimsical memorial of the Conquest is exhibited in the evening at the theatre. A popular drama is performed, entitled AVE MARIA, turning on a famous achievement of Hernando del Pulgar, surnamed "el de las Hazanas" (he of the exploits), a madcap warrior, the favorite hero of the populace of Granada. During the time of the siege, the young Moorish and Spanish cavaliers vied with each other in extravagant bravadoes. On one occasion this Hernando del Pulgar, at the head of a handful of followers, made a dash into Granada in the dead of the night, nailed the inscription of AVE MARIA with his dagger to the gate of the principal mosque, a token of having consecrated it to the Virgin, and effected his retreat in safety.

While the Moorish cavaliers admired this daring exploit, they felt bound to resent it. On the following day, therefore, Tarfe, one of the stoutest among them, paraded in front of the Christian army, dragging the tablet bearing the sacred inscription AVE MARIA, at his horse's tail. The cause of the Virgin was eagerly vindicated by Garcilaso de la Vega, who slew the Moor in single combat, and elevated the tablet in devotion and triumph at the end of his lance.

The drama founded on this exploit is prodigiously popular with the common people. Although it has been acted time out of mind, it never fails to draw crowds, who become completely lost in the delusions of the scene. When their favorite Pulgar strides about with many a mouthy speech, in the very midst of the Moorish capital, he is cheered with enthusiastic bravos; and when he nails the tablet to the door of the mosque, the theatre absolutely shakes with the thunders of applause. On the other hand, the unlucky actors who figure in the part of the Moors, have to bear the brunt of popular indignation, which at times equals that of the Hero of La Mancha, at the puppet-show of Gines de Passamonte; for, when the infidel Tarfe plucks down the tablet to tie it to his horse's tail, some of the audience rise in fury, and are ready to jump upon the stage to revenge this insult to the Virgin.

By the way, the actual lineal descendant of Hernando del Pulgar was the Marquis de Salar. As the legitimate representative of that madcap hero, and in commemoration and reward of this hero's exploit, above mentioned, he inherited the right to enter the cathedral on certain occasions, on horseback; to sit within the choir, and to put on his hat at the elevation of the host, though these privileges were often and obstinately contested by the clergy. I met him occasionally in society; he was young, of agreeable appearance and manners, with bright black eyes, in which appeared to lurk some of the fire of his ancestors. Among the paintings in the Vivarrambla, on the fete of Corpus Christi, were some depicting, in vivid style, the exploits of the family hero. An old gray-headed servant of the Pulgars shed tears on beholding them, and hurried home to inform the marquis. The eager zeal and enthusiasm of the old domestic only provoked a light laugh from his young master; whereupon, turning to the brother of the marquis, with that freedom allowed in Spain to old family servants, "Come, senor," cried he, "you are more considerate than your brother; come and see your ancestor in all his glory!"

In emulation of this great Dia de la Toma of Granada, almost every village and petty town of the mountains has its own anniversary, commemorating, with rustic pomp and uncouth ceremonial, its deliverance from the Moorish yoke. On these occasions, according to Mateo, a kind of resurrection takes place of ancient armor and weapons; great two-handed swords, ponderous arquebuses with matchlocks, and other warlike relics, treasured up from generation to generation, since the time of the Conquest; and happy the community that possesses some old piece of ordnance, peradventure one of the identical lombards used by the conquerors; it is kept thundering along the mountains all day long, provided the community can afford sufficient expenditure of powder.

In the course of the day, a kind of warlike drama is enacted. Some of the populace parade the streets, fitted out with the old armor, as champions of the faith. Others appear dressed up as Moorish warriors. A tent is pitched in the public square, inclosing an altar with an image of the Virgin. The Christian warriors approach to perform their devotions; the infidels surround the tent to prevent their entrance; a mock fight ensues; the combatants sometimes forget that they are merely playing a part, and dry blows of grievous weight are apt to be exchanged. The contest, however, invariably terminates in favor of the good cause. The Moors are defeated and taken prisoners. The image of the Virgin, rescued from thraldom, is elevated in triumph; a grand procession succeeds, in which the conquerors figure with great applause and vainglory; while their captives are led in chains, to the evident delight and edification of the spectators.

These celebrations are heavy drains on the treasuries of these petty communities, and have sometimes to be suspended for want of funds; but, when times grow better, or sufficient money has been hoarded for the purpose, they are resumed with new zeal and prodigality.

Mateo informed me that he had occasionally assisted at these fetes and taken a part in the combats, but always on the side of the true faith; "Porque senor," added the ragged descendant of the cardinal Ximenes, tapping his breast with something of an air, "porque senor, soy Cristiano viejo."

Washington Irving

Guide to Alhambra and Granada

Maribel's Guides For The Sophisticated Traveler
http://www.maribelsguides.com/

Granada

The capital city of the province of Granada, in the autonomous community of Andalusia, Spain. Granada is located at the foot of the Sierra Nevada mountains, at the confluence of four rivers, the Beiro, the Darro, the Genil and the Monachil. It sits at an average elevation of 738 metres above sea level, yet is only one hour by car from the Mediterranean coast, the Costa Tropical.

In the 2005 national census, the population of the city of Granada proper was 236,982, and the population of the entire urban area was estimated to be 472,638, ranking as the 13th-largest urban area of Spain. About 3.3% of the population did not hold Spanish citizenship, the largest number of these people (31%; or 1% of the total population) coming from South America. Its nearest airport is Federico García Lorca Granada-Jaén Airport.

Granada is a city in southern Spain's Andalusia region, in the foothills of the Sierra Nevada mountains. It's known for grand examples of medieval architecture dating to the Moorish occupation, especially the Alhambra. This sprawling hilltop fortress complex encompasses royal palaces, serene patios, and reflecting pools from the Nasrid dynasty, as well as the fountains and orchards of the Generalife gardens.

Why Visit?

This capital of Eastern Andalusia, with a population of 300,000, is blessed with both a stunning setting in the foothills of the Sierra Nevada and a fascinating history, straddling eastern and western civilizations - a city caught between oriental and occidental sensibilities. Its crown jewel, the Alhambra, moored above the city like a ship, is the greatest relic of Islamic Spain, the last stronghold of the Moorish empire and one of the world's most magical landmarks.

When to visit?

Almost anytime! Granada is a destination suitable, really, for all four seasons. In winter, you'll find fewer crowds, yet the temperatures are still warm enough for pleasant touring; spring brings the heavenly scents of jasmine and myrtle, making a tour of the Generalife gardens an absolute delight; fall is pleasantly cool with fewer crowds; late June - early July brings the added attraction of the prestigious International Festival of Music and Dance, while mid-July through August are the least pleasant months to visit due to the soaring heat and the almost unbearable tourist hordes.

Festivals

El Día de la Toma
Festival commemorating the anniversary of the capture of the city by the Catholic Monarchs and subsequent expulsion of the Moors – January 2.San Cecilio - City's patron saint's day – Pilgrimage to Sacromonte, first Sunday of February.

Las Cruces de Mayo (on and around May 3)
Some 30 + enormous crosses made of flowers are installed in the city's squares by various brotherhoods that compete to win a prize for the best-decorated and most elaborate cross. In each square a temporary bar is also set up for drinks and tapas and of course, spontaneous music and flamenco dancing at night.

Corpus Christi (end of May, early June)
Depending on when Easter falls in the calendar - a moveable feast, is celebrated on the Thursday after Trinity Sunday.
Although Corpus Christi is celebrated everywhere in Andalucía, it is celebrated most exuberantly in Granada with religious parades, concerts, bullfights and flamenco, and a fairground, El Ferial, set up at the edge of the city, which comes alive each night for an entire week.
The seven-day bullfighting Feria del Corpus coincides with the celebration of Corpus Christi and where the most prestigious matadors in Spain perform in the Plaza de Toros (bullring) at the western end of the city.

International Muséo and Dance Festival
(Third week of June through first week of July)
Note for would be festival-attendees: Due to the festival's enormous prestige throughout Europe, tickets for most performances are extremely difficult to obtain. They are put on sale (online) on a date in mid-April, (in '09 this magic date was April 18), and tickets to the high-status events can sell out by the end of the day! If you do have your heart set on attending an event, note the date and time on your calendar and be prepared to attempt a purchase at the hour in Granada when the box office opens!

The two major venues are the Generalife gardens (for dance) and the circular courtyard of the Palace of Charles V (for orchestra-soloists). But included in each year's program are free concerts in the Hospital Real at 12:30 pm and in the patio of El Corral del Carbón at 8:30 pm. Since seating is limited be sure to arrive quite early.

How to reach Granada

Arriving by AirFrom the UK
There are flights to the Granada-Jaén Federico García Lorca airport from Liverpool, London Gatwick and Stansted, Nottingham and East Midlands.

From the US
Fly from your home airport in the US to Madrid or Barcelona.

From within Spain
- *Madrid*: Iberia or Spanair flight (40 minutes) to Granada.
- *Barcelona*: Vueling, Iberia, Click Air and Spanair fly direct.
- *Girona:* Ryanair direct
- *Palma de Mallorca:* Air Europe direct

Arriving by Train From Madrid
The National Railway of Spain, **Renfe** (www.renfe.es), currently offers only two daily Altaria trains, taking 4 hr. 30 minutes. Deeply discounted Web (60% off) and Estrella (40% off) are available if ticket is purchased a minimum of 15 days (Web) or 7 days (Estrella) prior to departure. Non-refundable. The comfortable Altaria trains offer two classes of service, *turista* (tourist class) and *preferente* or business class with meal served along with wines and cordials plus access to the VIP lounge in Madrid's Atocha station. Web fares are not available in *preferente* class.

From Seville
Renfe offers 4 Regional trains; the ride takes 3 hours.

From Barcelona
Renfe has only 2 daily trains to Granada, either an 11 hr. 10 min. long ride on the ARCO, which departs in the morning, or the overnight Trenhotel. From Barcelona it is much better (and quite cheap) to fly! Granada's train station is located on Avenida Andalucía, 1.5 km west of the city center, right off Avenida de la Constitución. From there you can take a public bus (4,6,7,9 or 11) from Avda Constitución to the center, or take a taxi for about 5€.

Arriving by Bus From Seville
The best, most economical and comfortable mode of transport to Granada is via the **Alsina Graells** bus, a division of Alsa (www.alsa.es), which departs from Seville's Prado-San Sebastian bus station. There are eight daily departures, seven are non-stop and one makes an intermediary stop in Antequera. Buses arrive at Granada's main bus station on the Carretera de Jaén, 3 km northwest of the city center. The same company offers bus service to Granada from *Córdoba* and *Málaga*. City bus #3 runs from the station to the

city center. Taxi fare from the station to a downtown hotel is approximately €7.

From Madrid – Enatcar,
Another division of Alsa, plies this route with regular and Supra (express; non-stop) service daily from the Estación Sur de Autobuses. Morning buses currently depart at 7:30, 8:00 (Supra), 8:30, 10:30 and 11:30. The one-way fare is 15.66€ for normal service, 30.55€ for non-stop. A normal trip takes 5 hours, while non- stop service shaves 45 minutes from the ride.

Transportation
Granada Airport to Downtown

By Bus
Autocares José González operates the service between the airport, which is located 17 km outside the city, and downtown Granada, and its blue (unlike the city's red) buses are timed to meet all flights.

After collecting your luggage, exit the double doors and take a right, walk to the end of the hall and out a second set of double doors and look to your left. You'll see the bus waiting (well beyond the taxi stand). Stash your luggage in the underbelly, board and buy your €3 ticket from the bus driver. Buses will wait for all delayed flights.

The airport bus makes five intermediary stops before reaching the end of its route at the Palace of Congresses. The entire trip takes between 40 - 45 minutes. If you are staying at a downtown hotel, you can get off at stop 4, on the Gran Vía de Colón (best). If your hotel is located in the Albaicín or on the Alhambra hill, just hail a taxi from the stop on the Gran Vía.

To return to the airport for your flight home, the bus departs from the Paseo del Violón daily at 5:45, 6:30, 7:40, 8:40, 9:45, 10:45, 11:45, 12:45, 13:45, 14:45, 16:00, 17:00,18:00, 18:45, 19:45 and 20:30. Be sure to check the current schedule at: www.autocaresjosegonzalez.com.

By Taxi
Estimated taxi fares are as follows: to downtown, 25€; to the Alhambra, 28€; to the Albaicín, 28€; to the Sierra Nevada, 60€.

By Rental Car
The major players, Avis, Europcar, Hertz and Atesa have counters at the airport, but I strongly advise you **not** to keep a car in Granada. Negotiating the city traffic and poor signage can be a nightmare, even for veteran Spain travelers. A car in the city will be an albatross for you, a genuine handicap.

If you must arrive by car, I urge you to choose a hotel on the Alhambra hill for its ease of access and your driver's peace of mind. To reach the Alhambra area hotels, one avoids all city traffic completely, by taking the Carretera de Circunvalación or

Ronda Sur, which circumvents the downtown and brings traffic through a tunnel and directly up to the Alhambra. Just follow the purple Alhambra signs.

You'll find downtown parking garages few and far between, cost from 15€ - 20€ per day, there is **no** parking for most Albaicín hotels and only a few downtown hotels, such as the large convention-type hotels, offer their own on-site garages. But again, finding ones

way to a downtown hotel is a vexing, stress-inducing chore for most tourists, and motorcycle traffic adds to the frustration and confusion.

If you'll already chosen a downtown hotel that does not have an on-site garage, the simplest way to reach downtown is to take the "Centro-Recogidas" exit. Along Calle Recogidas you'll find an underground garage on your left. At the top of Calle Recogidas turn right on to Acera del Darro, where you'll see the central post office. There will be an underground garage on your left after the post office (*Correos*).

Public Transportation

Please do not attempt to drive - leave the navigating to the professionals!

Guidebook quotations regarding driving in downtown Granada:

> **Frommer's:** *"It's impossible to get around Granada by driving."*
> **Footprint Andalucía:** *"If arriving by car, the best option is to stash it as soon as possible."*
> **Time Out: Andalucía:** *"The city is a nightmare to negotiate by car (and has been deliberately made so). Finding a parking space in the center is all but impossible, so head straight for a car park."*
> **Thomas Cook:** *"The old center is only open to local traffic or for hotel access during certain hours of the day. Parking is a problem, so if you plan to stay overnight make sure that your hotel has parking facilities...it can cost as much as the accommodation in some places."*
> **Insight Guides:** *"the center of the city is noisy, the narrow streets being simply incapable of coping with the volume of traffic which churns through at all hours of the day and night. The visitor who arrives by car may well find himself swept through and out the other side without either having recognized the center of the town or seen a trace of its much-vaunted monuments."*
> **Rick Steves:** *"Driving in Granada's historic center is restricted to buses, taxis and tourists with hotel reservations. Signs are posted to this effect, and entrance is strictly controlled. Getting into the old center and finding your hotel or parking garage is a major frustration because of the strict controls and one way streets...Given all the restrictions, it is difficult to drive into Granada even when you know the system."*

Since downtown Granada is extremely congested, many streets are blocked off to vehicular traffic other than taxis and buses, and the layout is labyrinthine in nature, I strongly suggest that you avail yourself of the excellent and easy to use bus system. The red city buses, run by Transportes Rober, are inexpensive and compact enough to handle the narrow streets. A single ride costs €1.10 or a booklet of 7 bus tickets, which can be shared, costs 5€. Buy your single ticket or booklet from the driver, who accepts bills (www.transportesrober.es).

For the short-term visitor, the red minibuses with only about ten seats, designated **Alhambrabús**, are the most efficient way of seeing the city's major attractions. These minibuses provide service to the Alhambra hill from 7:15 am until 11:00 pm. Buses **30** and **32** run from downtown to the Alhambra (the 32 bus making a swing through the Albaicín) and the bus **31** runs from the Plaza Nueva to the Albaicín only. Bus **34** detours east to Sacromonte. The fare for the minibuses is one euro. City bus **8** runs to the Monasterio de la Cartuja. City bus **3** and **33** go to the bus station. Buses **3** and **9** run from the train station, down the Avenida de la Constitución to the cathedral. A taxi fare within the city should cost between 5€ - 8€.

Granada Tourist Office
Plaza de Mariana Pineda, 10, is open Monday - Friday 9:30 – 7:00 and Saturday from 10:00 – 2:00. This is the regional tourist office for the city and Granada province as well (www.turismodegranada.org).

Andalucía Tourist Office
Can be found at Calle Santa Ana, 4, near the Plaza Nueva and is open from 9:00 - 7:30 Monday – Friday, Saturday from 10:00 - 7:30 and Sunday from 10:00 – 2:00.

Granada's Highlights

The "not to miss" tourist attractions
In order of importance and cultural interest for the first time visitor.

ALHAMBRA *(from the Arabic "Al Qal'a al-Hamra" - Red Fort)*

The Alhambra Palace was one of the greatest architectural wonders of the world when it was created in the 13th and 14th centuries and remains so today. It is unlikely that any future civilisation will ever be able to match the magnificence and mysticism of the Alhambra Palace - truly an extraordinary fairytale palace.
The Alhambra is a unique creation spawned from the gold coffers of Moorish sultans the creative minds of poets and philosophers and the agony of slave labour

Wars, sieges and years of neglect have failed to detract from the allure of the Alhambra Palace which continues to attract millions of visitors each year to a hilltop that overlooks the city of Granada.

It was the last and most splendid of all the Arabian palaces to be built in Spain during 700 years of Moorish domination. The Moors were vastly superior to their European enemies in all areas of culture and the Alhambra Palace became a glorious symbol of not only their wealth and power but also their unsurpassable artistic and architectural skills.

The palace was constructed as both a fortress and royal residence for the sultans after the Christians recaptured Cordoba, which was the former capital of the mighty Western Islamic empire known as El Andalus.

From the mid-1200s onwards, the Moorish Nasrid Dynasty set about establishing a citadel and palace the like of which the world had never seen before. On the hilltop site of an existing 10th century Arab fortress, the sultans brought together their empire's greatest minds and most talented craftsmen to fashion an exotic array of exquisitely decorated palaces and courtyards within the walls of a castle designed to withstand the might of the Christian armies.

Visit the Alhambra today and you'll still find a mesmerising mixture of the most intricate tilework, filigree decoration and mosaics within its royal rooms and shaded courtyards. A sensual blend of bubbling fountains, dark green pools, white marble floors and enchanting passage ways draw you back through the centuries to a time and place where sultans once ruled and relaxed on silken cushions while naked beauties danced for them (accompanied by blind musicians!)

Jewels in the crown of the Alhambra include the legendary Court of the Lions with its famous fountain, the Hall of the Kings and Hall of the Queens, the royal baths and the magnificent Hall of the Two Sisters lavishly decorated with gold and lapis lazuli.

Within the grounds of the Alhambra lies the most popular Parador hotel in Spain, housed within a 15th century covent which was part of the Moorish palace before being captured by the Christians in 1492. The hotel houses the former chapel where the crusading Catholic monarchs Isabella and Ferdinand were temporarily buried before being moved to their final resting place in Granada's Capilla Real. Be warned that if you want to stay in this particular Parador you'll probably have to book several months in advance.

In July and August, the Alhambra Palace is the main venue for the annual International Festival of Music and Dance which attracts some of the world's top orchestras, flamenco performers and ballet companies.

If you plan to visit in high season it's worth securing an entrance ticket in advance because this is one of Spain's top tourist attractions and numbers are restricted. This guide will not attempt to relate the history or to give a detailed room-to-room description of all the wonders of this astonishing World Heritage Site, Spain's most visited tourist attraction.

The complex is divided into four main components: the original 13th century fortress, or **Alcazaba**, the Royal Nasrid Palace or **Palacios Nazaríes** - also called the Casa Real, the **Generalife**, the sultans' summer palace and gardens (all part of your ticket) and "the imperial intrusion" to the Moorish complex, the 16th century Renaissance **Palace of Charles V**, which is free-no ticket required. To visit the first **three** components, one needs to purchase a combined ticket, and it is imperative that one purchases this ticket **well in advance** during the summer months and school holidays.

With more than 2 million visitors each year, the Alhambra is the most popular tourist attraction in Spain. Because entrance to the complex is limited to only 7,250 visitors (6,050 in winter) each day, with 300 visitors per half-hour time slot, and with only 400 admitted for the night visit, **I strongly recommend** that you purchase your Alhambra tickets online at **Alhambra-guide.com**, and well ahead of your visit-for the summer high season and for all school holidays, up to **3** months or **90 days** in advance.

Only 1,800 tickets are sold daily at the box office, and during the high season, one must be in line by 7 am for even a chance to secure a ticket for that day; therefore, advanced booking is preferable, even essential. Visit Alhambra-guide.com for bookings. And during the summer months, because of the intense heat, I also urge you to choose the very first entrance slot, at 8:30 am, for your timed ticket, as the bus tour crowds arrive at around 10 am, and the mid-day heat can make for exhausting touring.

In the winter months, an afternoon visit can be pleasant, with fewer crowds, but be sure to choose a timed slot for the Nasrid Palace entrance **no later** than 4:00 - 4:30 pm, because the complex closes at 6:00 pm November - February.

If you choose this time slot, while waiting your timed entrance to the Nasrid Palaces between 2:00 – 4:00 pm, you can visit the Alcazaba military fortress, the Generalife summer palace and gardens, or Charles V's Palace (and the two museums lying within) and the remainder of the complex. You will need at least 3 1/2 to 4 hours to do justice to the entire site.

Also there are no public dining facilities (café's and restaurants) within the complex itself, only vending machines for water, soft drinks and sandwiches at the Entrance Pavilion and a bar/café kiosk for the same near the Alcazaba, adjacent to the Puerta del Vino (Wine Gate). Therefore, I also suggest that visitors arm themselves with bottled water in the scorching summer months.

Visitors must deposit backpacks and bags larger than 35 cm. in the checkroom at the Entrance Pavilion.

Again, your bar coded ticket will be scanned at **three** entrances secured by turnstiles:

- At the door to the Palacios Nazaríes
- At the gate which leads to the Generalife summer palace and gardens
- At the entrance to the Alcazaba fortress. Entrance to the courtyard of the Palace of Chares V and entrance to the 17th century church, Iglesia de Santa María de la Alhambra, and Mosque baths, Baños de la Mezquita, **do not** require the Alhambra ticket, nor does strolling the Calle Real de la Alhambra, where you will find the souvenir shops, bookstore, Hotel América and the Parador. Plus you may also wander freely around the Plaza de los Aljibes in front of the Alcazaba and other public squares.

  Two museums are housed within the **Palace of Charles V**, one of which charges an entrance fee (except to EU members).

1. The excellent **Museum of the Alhambra** on the ground floor contains an impressive collection of Hispano-Muslim art, such as the original tiles and plaster arabesques from the palace, beautiful ceramics and most importantly, one of the twelve lions from the Courtyard of the Lions, which have all been removed for a major cleaning and restoration. I urge you not to miss this fine museum. The restoration of one of the twelve lions has been completed, and he appears much more beautiful, more slender and svelte, and is displayed along with an interesting slide-show explanation of the painstaking restoration process. Open Tuesday - Saturday 9:00 - 2:30. Closed Sunday and Mondays, free on holidays,

2. The **Museo de Bellas Artes** (Fine Arts Museum) is located on the top floor of the palace and consists of a collection of religious paintings from various Granada churches, including works by Granada native son, Alonso Cano, sometimes referred to as the Spanish Michelangelo (as he was a 17th century painter, sculptor and architect). *This museum, for me, is*

not a "must see". Open Tuesday from 2:30 – 6:00 (8:00 in the summer), Wednesday - Saturday 9:00 – 6:00 (8:00 in the summer) and Sundays 9:00 - 2:30. Closed Monday. Admission: 1.50€ (Free to EU members).

Note: As of late, substantial areas of the Nasrid Palaces are being temporarily closed to visitors due to extensive renovations, particularly during the winter months. On our last visit in February, the Sala del Rey, the Charles V chambers (inhabited by Washington Irving in 1892) and the hammam, **Baños Arabes**, were all under restoration and closed to the public.

Reaching the Alhambra

Arriving by car
If you drive to the Alhambra from outside Granada, make sure to follow the Ronda Sur-Carretera de Circunvalación signs that will take you up the hill and lead you directly to the very large parking lots on the Avenida de los Alixares, across from the Hotel Guadalupe and Hotel Alixares, just a short distance uphill from the ticket office.

Arriving by bus
To reach the Alhambra by bus from downtown, take the #30 or #32 red Alhambra minibus (fare: 1€), which runs approximately every 10 min., departing from the Plaza Nueva. It stops just below the ticket office.

Arriving by taxi
A ride from the taxi stand at the Plaza Nueva to the Entrance Pavilion should cost around 4€.

Arriving on foot
If you plan to walk up to the Alhambra from downtown, allow 30 minutes to reach the complex. The most direct route will take you up the steep Cuesta de Gomérez, which begins at the Plaza Nueva leading up through the woods to the Puerta de las Granadas. Immediately after the Puerta de las Granadas, turn left up the Cuesta Empedrada path to the fountain, Pilar de Carlos V. If you already have your ticket, there's no need to continue walking up to the ticket office at the official Entrance Pavilion. After the fountain take a sharp left and enter the Alhambra through the Puerta de la Justicia (Gate of Justice). There's an Information stand a short distance inside this gate where you can pick up a map of the grounds. If you do need to pick up your tickets (reserved on line) at the Servi Caixa machines, continue outside the Alhambra walls from the Pilar de Carlos V fountain, a distance of about 600 meters, to the Entrance Pavilion, Pabellón de Acceso. Remember that it is a good 15- minute walk from the Entrance Pavilion to the entrance to the Nasrid Palaces. So be sure to arrive at the Entrance Pavilion with ample time to walk down to the palace before your allotted half-hour slot for entry expires.

Walking back to downtown

There is a delightful walk back down into town by way of the Cuesta de los Chinos ("chinos" referring to the splinter stones that pave the way). It is also called Cuesta del Rey Chico (the "rey chico" being Boabdil, the last Nasrid King of Granada). At La Mimbre restaurant look for the sign pointing the way. This pathway will take you back down into town, running along the ramparts of the Alcazaba fortress on your left, but don't attempt this walk without very sturdy, thick-soled shoes, as you will be walking on large, irregular stones, the path is steep and the going is slow. It will deposit you at the Paseo de los Tristes, which runs along the Darro river, and from there you can either continue your walk up into the ancient Arab quarter of the Albaicín by turning right and walking up the Cuesta Chapiz, or turn left and walk down the Paseo de los Tristes, which will lead you to the Plaza Nueva and monumental downtown Granada.

The Cerro del Sol

A complex on the high plateau which overlooks the town to the south east. It includes the superb palace of Granada's Moorish kings, which was principally under the Nasrite rulers Yusuf I (1333-54) and Mohammed V (1354-91). Massive towers and gates surround the palace complex emphasizing its fortress-like character; there are also ring walls and the remains of the Alcazaba.

The Alcazaba was built by Mohammed V in shimmering red stone which led to the description 'Calat Alhambra' (Red Castle).

From the top of the Torre de la Vela, which is 29 meters (87 ft.) high, you get a panoramic view across the Sierra Nevada. The road up into the Alhambra park passes through the Puerta de las Granadas, a triumphal arch decorated with three pomegranates and designed by Pedro Machuca. To the right, on Monte Mauror, the 12th century Torres Bermejas can be seen; this is part of the fortification that links with the Alcazaba.

Further on you arrive at the Puerta de la Justicia, built by Yusuf I in 1348. Above the gate's first horseshoe arch there is a carved hand that symbolizes its defence against evil. The second horseshoe arch is decorated with many Arab inscriptions and beautiful blue and green azulejos.

After four right-angled bends (for reasons of defence), you arrive at the entrance to the Alhambra Palace itself. Nearby the Renaissance fountain (1545) dates from the time of Charles V and is the work of Pedro Machuca. The 14th century Puerta del Vino leads to the Plaza de los Aljibes *('Square of Wells')*.

The 'Gate of Wine' displays the Nasrites' artistic style to great advantage. To the west of the square there are the former buildings of the Alcazaba; to the east there is the Palace of Charles V and to the north the Palacio Arabe *(the Alhambra Palace)*.

The Alcazaba is enclosed by ramparts and several of its towers still survive. The Torre de la Vela is the most significant and dominates a magnificent panorama of the city and surrounding areas.

Also of interest are the Torre del Homenaje *(the Keep)*, Torre Quebrada and Torre del Adarguero. The Puerta de la Tahona, in the tower of the same name, affords access to the royal palaces.

The Mexuar palace was originally given over to administrative and judicial affairs; and the Royal Council used to meet here. Although now in a deficient state of repair, the main section is a hall centred around four columns and a modern fountain; this was used as a chapel from the 18th century until the 20th.

The north facade serves as a portico for the Cuarto Dorado *('Golden Room')*.

The facade on the other side of the Mexuar is called the Serrallo front, its artistic eaves are remarkable.

After the Serrallo facade, the you reach the Patio de los Arrayanes *('Court of Myrtles')*, also known as Patio de la Alberca, *del Estanque* or *de los Mirtos*, with a magnificent pool in the centre. Its arches are semicircular, with a voussoired structure. Special mention should be made of the wooden ceiling in the north gallery and the alabaster lamp-stands, with ceramics at the back, located in the jambs of the doorway.

The Sala de la Barca is between the portico and the Throne Room; its name derives from the inverted hull of a boat that adorns the ceiling.

The Salon de Embajadores *('Ambassadors' Hall')*, also known as de Comares, is next, this was the centre of political and diplomatic life. Although it was once superbly decorated, it now retains only its artistic and architectural design.

Continuing towrads the baths, the visitor will reach the Patio de la Reja *('Court of the Ruling')* with its fountain and cypress trees.

Next is the Jardin de Lindaja *('Lindaraxa's Garden')*, which does not correspond to the moorish period, but dates from the 16th century. It was designed to embellish the courtyard onto which Charles V's room opened. A post-reconquest fountain with an Arab basin stands in the centre.

The Banos Reales *('Royal Baths')* stand next to Lindaraxa's Garden, displaying polychromatic decoration, predominately blue, green, gold and red in the main room, where there is also a small 16th century fountain. The Royal Baths comprises of three further sections:

The Tocador de la Reina ('Queen's Boudoir') is between the Ambassadors'Hall and the Harem. This room was built for the *Empress Isabella* and displays outstanding fresco paintings on the walls. By the door to one of the Emperor's rooms there is a tablet recalling that Washington Irving, the author of The Alhambra, once stayed there.

The artistically decorated Sala de los Ajimeces *('Hall of Mullioned Windows')* id the first of the rooms making up the Harem and its ceiling was restored in the 16th century. The Sala de las Dos Hermanas *('Hall of the Two Sisters')* is beyond Lindaraxa's Balcony. Boabdil's mother lived here after being repudiated by Muley Hacen. The decoration is superb and the dome harmonious.

The name of the Patio de los Leones *('Court of Lions')* is due to the twelve figures of lions that support the fountain in the centre. This rectangular courtyard, built in the reign of Mohammed V, is surrounded by a gallery supported by 124 elegant white marble columns.

The Sala de los Reyes, also called *de la Justicia ('Hall of Kings/Justice')*, lies to the east of the Court of Lions. It was a Christian church from the time that the royal mosque disappeared until the construction of the church of Santa Maria de la Alhambra and is adorned by a painting of ten Moorish kings assembled in a meeting.

The Sala de los Abencerrajes (*'Hall of the Abencerrages'*) is another important room as all of the children of Muley Abul Hassan were executed here upon marrying Zoraida.

The last room in the Harem is the Sala de los Mocarabes (mocarabe - carpenter´s design of interlaced prisms), which now displays baroque decoration on the ceiling.

Other interesting sights to see at the Alhambra Palace in Granada
- Remains of the Alhambra´s royal cemetery
- Partal or Torre de las Damas (*'Ladies Tower'*)
- The towers known as de los Picos (named after its pointed crenellations)
    - del Cadi ('of the Judge')
    - de la Cautiva ('of the Prisoner')
    - de las Infantas ('of the Princesses')
- Generalife Gardens
- Palacio de Carlos V
- Museo Nacional de Arte Hispano-Musulman ('The National Museum of Hispano-Muslim Art')
- Museo Provincial de Bellas Artes ('The Fine Arts Museum of the Province')
- The Alcazaba
- The Royal Palaces
- Church of Santa Maria of the Alhambra

Other Attractions

The Royal Chapel

Adjoining Granada's cathedral, this is downtown Granada's most outstanding Christian building. The Catholic Monarchs, Fernando and Isabel commissioned it after the fall of Moorish Granada as their own mausoleum. They had originally planned to be interred in Toledo but after their victory against the Moors they gave orders to Enrique Egas for the construction of this burial chapel, begun in 1506.

Egas built the chapel in the elaborate and delicate Isabelline Gothic style, but it wasn't finished until 1521, several years after their deaths, during the reign of their grandson, Charles V. The Monarchs were temporarily buried in the Convento de San Francisco at the Alhambra, now the Parador, until the completion of the Capilla Real. The King and Queen's magnificently carved Carrera marble sarcophagi, the work of Bartolomé Ordóñez, are found next to those of their daughter, Joan the Mad (mother of Charles V), and her husband, Philip the Fair. The lower two are those of the King and Queen; those of Felipe and Juana lie higher, some say, perhaps because Felipe was the son of the Holy Roman Emperor Maximilian. The actual small and simple lead coffins, containing their remains, lie in the crypt below, along with the coffin of Juana and Felipe's only child. The magnificent central altarpiece of the Chapel depicts the fall of Granada with Boabdil, the last Moorish ruler, handing over the keys to the city.
Note: it's very much an open question whether the actual remains are still here, as the coffins were opened and desecrated during the Napoleonic invasion in 1812.

The sacristy of the Royal Chapel **should not be missed**. It's an impressive museum containing, among other gems, Isabel's crown and scepter, her ornate jewelry chest, mirror, illuminated missal, Fernando's sword and the Kings' personal, mostly Hispano- Flemish, art collection including works by van der Weyen and Hans Memling.
The Royal Chapel is open from April to October from 10:30 – 1:00 and from 4:00 – 7:00. From November - March it's open from 10:30 – 1:00 and 3:30 – 6:00, and on Sundays from 11:00 – 1:00 and 3:30 – 6:00. Closed Good Friday, December 25, January 1. Admission: 3€, but is free with Bono Turístico.

Cathedral (*downtown Granada*)

The cavernous cathedral, built on the site of the demolished Great Mosque, was begun in 1518 in Gothic style, but was not finished until 1563. The architect, Diego Siloe, who replaced Enrique Egas five years after its start, made changes to the design, introducing the Renaissance style to the building. In the Capilla Mayor, note the praying figures of Fernando and Isabel, works by native son Pedro de Mena.
Open Monday - Saturday from 10:45 - 1:30 and 3:30 - 6:30. On Sundays it is only open for visits from 3:30 - 6:30. The main entrance can be found on Gran Vía de Colón.

Monasterio de la Cartuja *(downtown Granada)*

This over-the-top, lavishly, wildly, flamboyantly Baroque extravaganza, the "Sistine Chapel of Baroque Art", lies two km northwest of the city, easily reachable by #8 bus, which runs along the Gran Vía (www.diocesisgranada.org). It's often been described as the Christian answer to the Alhambra, their attempt to upstage the Moors in grandiosity. A Spanish writer describes the high altar as a "motionless architectural earthquake". For art lovers, missing the Cartuja in Granada would be akin to visiting Rome and failing to see the Vatican.
Open daily from November – March 10:00 – 1:00 and 3:30 – 6:00. From April - October it is open from 10:00 – 1:00 and 4:00 – 8:00. However, on Sundays and holidays it only opens from 10:00 - noon. Admission: 3,50€.

Monasterio de San Jerónimo *(downtown Granada)*

Diego de Siloé, who took over the construction of Granada's cathedral, and who is known for his fine Plateresque work, designed this 16th century monastery, located 500 meters west of the cathedral on Calle Rector López Argüeta. The church contains a beautiful two-tiered cloister and inside the ornately frescoed church, the tomb of Gonzalo Fernández de Córdoba, the Gran Capitán, who won many victories in Italy for the Catholic Monarchs.
Open April - October from 10:00 - 1:30 and 4:00 - 7:30. From November – March it's from 10:00 - 1:30 and from 3:00 - 6:30. Open Sundays from 10:00 - noon only. Admission: 3€.

El Albaizín

This fascinating, labyrinth-like quarter takes its name, some scholars say, from the Arabic "Rabad el-Bayyazin", which means "gate of the falconers" or it may refer to the "neighborhood of Baeza, as the former inhabitants of the Al Andalus town of Baeza settled here in Granada in 1227 after Baeza was re-conquered by the Christians.
A daylight stroll through the city's ancient Islamic quarter, the oldest section of town, which covers the slope directly facing the Alhambra, is a must for all visitors. Here is where the Moors built their first fortress, numerous mosques, and is the refuge where they retreated after the Christian Re-Conquest until they were finally driven out for good in 1609. This former Arab ghetto is a dense medina-like network of narrow and cramped, steep and winding cobbled streets, dead ends and little squares where getting lost is inevitable. As you walk along its streets and into its many squares, you'll be rewarded at every turn with stunning vistas of the Alhambra looming across the way on the Al-Sabika hill. The Albaicín area, once scruffy and semi-abandoned, is gradually gentrifying, particularly with the opening of small boutique hotels, restaurants-with- views in typical whitewashed cármenes, Arab teahouses, halal grocers and "Little Morocco" - a souk-like bazaar of leather and trinket shops in the lower quarter. The lower section is now inhabited by new Spanish Muslims, Moroccan and Algerian immigrants and New Age types.

You can spend a couple of hours soaking up the flavor of this quarter or spend the entire day lost in its innumerable nooks and crannies.

What is a Carmen? A whitewashed villa perched on a hill and hidden behind a tall white wall, surrounded by cypress tress, with murmuring fountains, terraced gardens planted with fruit trees and filled with flowing bougainvillea. There are more cármenes here in the Albaicín than in any other quarter of Granada. The 17th century poet, Pedro Soto de Rojas, wrote of them in his book entitled: "a paradise closed to many, gardens open to few". The 20th century Granadine poet, Federico García Lorca wrote: "to live on a different plane, in a Carmen - all the rest is a waste of time!"

Sacromonte

This desert-like, prickly pear-covered hillside opposite the Generalife gardens is riddled with troglodyte dwellings, once inhabited by gypsy (Gitano) families who were forced out in the floods of 1968 and is now the home largely to hippies with a scattering of gypsies who have returned. These gypsy families perform **zambras** (flamenco dances) in their cave-homes in the evenings, performances geared solely to tourists. Most of these *zambra* caves have the reputation of being classic "rip off joints" best to be avoided. I would tour this quarter only during the day. A walk through Sacromonte can be added to the above recommended walking tour of El Albaicín, simply by detouring east at the intersection of the **Cuesta del Chapiz** and **Camino de Sacromonte**. Sacromonte has
only one road, which curves around the hillside. The visitor leaves the city behind and enters a strange and very arid landscape where the only buildings of note are the caves dug out of the hillside.
If you'd like to see a cave replica, the **Center for the Interpretation of Sacromonte- Museo Cuevas del Sacromonte** is a type of ethnographic museum with ten caves displaying gypsy crafts (basketry work, pottery, metalwork, weaving) and the cave dwellers' way of life. To reach the center you'll need to climb 300 meters up the steep hill, **Barranco de los Negros**, from the #34 bus stop and Venta El Gallo restaurant at the end of the Camino del Monte (an extension of Camino de Sacromonte - the main drag). The visit takes about an hour. Admission fee: 5€. It opens Tuesday through Sunday, from April to October from 10:00 – 2:00 and 5:00 – 9:00. From November through March it is open from 10:00 – 2:00 and 4:00 – 7:00. Closed on Monday.
To reach Sacromonte by bus, take the #34 from the Plaza Nueva, which departs every hour from 7:30 am - 8:30 pm. But you will still need to make the 300-meter climb up to visit the Museo Cuevas (www.sacromontegranada.com).

Museo Arqueológico

The Casa de Castril, a Renaissance mansion with ornate Plateresque facade on the Carrera del Darro, is the setting for Granada's archeological museum housing artifacts from the Paleolithic age to the Islamic period. In room No. 4, upstairs, you'll find a stunning collection of alabaster burial urns. Open 9:00 - 8:30, but on Tuesdays from 2:30 – 8:00 only and on Sunday from 9:00 - 2:30. Closed Monday. Admission: €1.50 (free to EU citizens)

El Bañuelo-Baños Arabes (*downtown Granada*)

These brick vaulted 11th century Moorish baths are considered the best preserved in Spain. Note the star-shaped openings in the vaulting. During the Moorish occupation of Granada there was a bath on every street of the Albaicín, the Moors believing that cleanliness was next to godliness. Open Tuesday - Saturday from 10:00 – 2:00. Admission is free. Closed Sunday and Monday.

Fundación Rodríguez-Acosta (*Alhambra hill*)

This foundation-museum (www.fundacionrodriguezacosta.com) overlooking the city is a private non-profit organization founded in 1941 after the death of Granadino painter José María Rodríguez-Acosta who established the guidelines to the foundation and left his private collection to it. The foundation is housed in a beautiful Carmen on the Alhambra hill near the Torres Bermejas (just below the Hotel Alhambra Palace) and has spectacular gardens and equally spectacular views of Granada. It was declared a National Monument in 1982. Inside you'll find the Gómez-Moreno museum with a collection of valuable paintings by Zurbarán, Sorolla, Murillo and Fortuny along with archeological finds. Open Wednesday - Sunday from 10:00 – 2:00. Closed Monday, Tuesday, December 24, 25, 31 and January 1, plus other local holidays. Those who present their Alhambra ticket will receive a 50% discount on price of admission. Entrance: 4€.
You can reach the Foundation on the #30 or #32 red Alhambra microbus, getting off at the stop in front of the Hotel Alhambra Palace and walking down about 50 meters to the entrance to the Carmen.
The view of Granada from the Fundación Rodríguez-Acosta from above the Carmen de la Alcubilla del Caracol

Campo de los Mártires *Alhambra hill*

This is an expansive and peaceful garden that offers lovely views of the city. During the Re-Conquest it served as a fortress where captured Christian soldiers were held as prisoners in dungeons tunneled within the rocks. Open in winter, Monday - Friday from 10:00 – 2:00, Saturday and Sunday from 10:00 - 6:00. Open in the summer, Monday - Friday from 10:00 – 2:00 and 6:00 – 8:00, Saturday and Sunday from 10:00 – 8:00. Closed August.

Casa-Museo de Manuel de Falla *(Alhambra hill)*

Located on Antequeruela Alta on the Alhambra hill, near the Alhambra Palace Hotel. For Spanish classical music lovers, this is the home of composer Manuel de Falla, who lived in Granada for almost twenty years. When he left the city for exile in Argentina in 1939, he left behind his personal belongings, including manuscripts, concert programs, press clippings, posters, photographs, correspondence and books. The city opened the composer's former home as a museum in 1965. Open Tuesday - Sunday from 10:00 – 2:00. In July and Aug it is only open Thursday - Sunday. Admission: 3€.

Centro de Arte José Guerrero *(downtown Granada)*

For contemporary art lovers, this is a small museum dedicated to the work of native son, abstract expressionist José Guerrero, a contemporary of Pollock and Rothko. It also houses temporary exhibits. It opens Tuesday - Saturday 11:00 – 2:00 and 5:00 – 9:00, and Sunday from 11:00 – 2:00. Closed Monday (www.centroguerrero.org).

Casa de los Tiros *(downtown Granada)*

On Calle Pavaneras, 19, the street leading from the Plaza Isabel la Católica to the Realejo neighborhood, this fortress-like 16th century Renaissance palace *("the House of the Shots" - from the musket barrels protruding from the facade)*, now houses a collection of Royal paintings and lithographs depicting Granada in the 19th century. It opens on Tuesday in the afternoon only from 2:30 - 8:30. From Wednesday – Saturday it is open from 9:00 - 8:30, and on Sunday from 9:00 - 2:30. Closed Monday. Admission: 1.50€. Free to EU citizens.

Following the literary footsteps of Federico García Lorca

Granada's most illustrious citizen, Federico García Lorca, was one of Spain's literary giants, a member of the Generation of 1927. Both a renowned poet and playwright, he was brutally assassinated by Franco's Falangist followers during the opening days of the Spanish Civil War. In July of 1936, García Lorca decided to postpone a planned trip to Mexico and instead spend the summer in Granada. Tragically, this was the moment when the city fell to Franco's troops, who launched a vendetta to hunt down and exterminate all those who openly sympathized with the Republican cause.

The poet sought refuge in the house of friend and fellow poet, Luis Rosales, but was discovered and dragged away on 16 August. **Viznar** is where García Lorca spent his final hours before facing the firing squad. Close to the town is the *Viznar Gorge* where it is thought that his remains, along with those of other Civil War victims, were buried.

Those who have studied his work may want to make the pilgrimage to these **three** sites in and around the city that honor his memory - the corners of his childhood, his youth and the place of his death:

1. **La Huerta de San Vicente - Casa Museo Federico García Lorca** was the family summer residence between 1926-1936, once outside of town but now found within the burgeoning city limits, having been swallowed up by the city. The city government has transformed this area into a formal park and garden and has opened the home as a museum. Here is where García Lorca produced some of his finest work, including Blood Wedding and Yerma. The family has returned the home to its original state, and half-hour tours are given Tuesday – Sunday. From April - September it is open from 10:00 - 12:30 and from 5:00 - 7:30. From October - March it is open 10:00 - 12:30 and 4:00 - 6:30. It is closed in the afternoons during July and August and on Mondays. Because guided tours are mandatory it's important to check the calendar at www.huertadesanvicente.com to make sure that a space is available on the tour of your choice. The guided tours are currently given at 10:15, 11:00, 11:45, 12:30, 5:15, 6:00, 6:45 and 7:30 only, Admission: 3€, but free on Wednesday.

2. García Lorca shrine lies 17 km. due west of the city in the village of **Fuente Vaqueros**. The **Museo Casa-Natal Federico García Lorca** is the writer's birthplace and where he spent his early years. Tours will show you drawings by the young Federico, school photos, manuscripts and memorabilia from performances of his plays. From October – March it is open from 10:00 – 1:00 and 4:00 – 6:00, and from April - June and in September it's open from 10:00 – 1:00 and 5:00 – 7:00. During July and August it is only open from 10:00 – 2:00. Closed on Mondays.

3. The final stop on the García Lorca memory trail is found outside the village of **Alfacar,** north of Granada, where tragically, the artist was executed on 18 August 1936. A memorial park has been created in the place where it is believed the poet was assassinated. A wall with fragments of his poems etched on blue painted ceramic tiles surrounds the main square.

The City's Best Dining Experiences

Compared to other gastronomically renowned Spanish cities, particularly those of the north, San Sebastián, Bilbao, Barcelona, and relative to the other two Andalusian members of the "Golden Triangle", Seville and Córdoba, Granada has never been highly regarded by gastronomes-in-the-know for its innovative dining. The ironic expression *"comer en Granada es poco o nada"* pretty much sums it up, according to gourmet critics, when comparing dining here to the culinary fame of the north, although Córdoba is actually considered among the food critics to be the "gourmet capital" of the South.

Granada residents love their traditional recipes and as a conservative dining lot, don't venture much beyond the tried and true. That said, it's possible to dine well in Granada, but I would choose the "tapas" route over white tablecloth dining, with a few notable exceptions. Granada's tapas bars are well known for maintaining the tradition of offering a complimentary tapa along with an order of an alcoholic drink (beer, wine) or a soft drink (but not water, juice or coffee). This tradition not only thrives here, but has also developed into an art form.

These free tapas can be a little dish of stew, a mini sandwich, a slice of omelet, tortilla, a little dish of Russian salad, all quite filling, which makes a traditional "tapas crawl" imminently affordable. With each round of drinks at the bar, you will be given a different complimentary tapa-the waiters remember what complimentary snacks you have already been served and vary your treats. But remember that this is a gift, so one shouldn't request a particular tapa, unless you're a regular, but rather just enjoy what is given. And make sure not to order food immediately along with your drink, but instead, wait and order after finishing your tapa(s) so as not to over-order.

Regional dishes of Granada and/or Andalucía

- **Berenjenas con miel** - *Breaded eggplant with honey.*
- **Habitas con jamón** - *Broad beans sautéed with little pieces of Serrano ham*
- **Jamón de Trevélez** - *Mountain cured Serrano ham from the Alpujarras - cured in caves in the highest village of the Iberian Peninsula.*
- **Remojón** - *A salad of cod, oranges, black olives, onions and tomatoes*
- **Pescaíto Frito** - *Lightly battered, fried" little fishes"*
- **Tortilla Sacromonte** - *An omelet named after the Abbey of Sacromonte, which in its original version contains lambs' brains and testicles.*
- **Choto al ajillo** – *Kid (goat) braised in white wine and garlic.*
- **Alboronía** - *A vegetable medley consisting of eggplant, tomatoes, green peppers and squash.*
- **Olla de San Antón** - *A stew of lima beans, blood sausage, pig's head or ear, bacon, dripping, thistles – whatever comes to hand in the cold weeks of mid-January when villagers gather together to celebrate the fiesta of San Antón. Also acts as a hangover cure after Christmas and the New Year...*
- **Perdices** - *The name for baked potatoes in Granada (also partridges).*
- **Piononos** - *A dessert from the town of Santa Fe, made with sponge cake, cream, burnt sugar, cinnamon-available in all the city's pastry shops.*

Dining with a View
On the Alhambra hill

Parador San Francisco
Without a doubt, the former 15th century convent, now a state run Parador, is the most romantic and serene spot to dine on the Alhambra grounds. A dinner on the terrace of the Parador with a direct view of the Generalife gardens while being serenaded by a classical guitarist, the scent of orange blossoms and jasmine in the

air, can be a lovely, romantic experience. However, you will hear mostly English (or German), in the background, as this Parador is extremely popular with and primarily filled up by foreign guests. The dining room does not take reservations for non-hotel guests (or did not prior to the renovation), so your best bet is to arrive a bit before 9:00 pm. (it opens for dinner at 8:00) and wait to be seated on the terrace. There are also terrace tables where one can enjoy a pre-dinner drink, so the wait can be quite pleasant.

I always opt for a regional specialty (menu is divided between regional dishes and standard continental fare) and choose the decently priced, 32.50€, three course "menú Parador", a good value given the magical setting. On the menu there will be seafood options as well as meat dishes. Two of my favorite regional dishes served here are the *habitas con jamón* (baby limas with ham) and the *berenjenas con miel* (eggplant with honey). And from the wine list I select the label designated "best wine at the best price", or the "market discovery", which has always proved to be a solid bet.

If ordering a-la-carte, you will be charged 1.87€ each for the olives, oil, amuse-bouche and breads placed at your table at the beginning of the meal (these are included in the set menu price). For information and reservations call: 958 221 440.

Carmen de San Miguel
This Carmen turned restaurant is located immediately below the Torres Bermejas and a short stroll up the street from the guesthouse Carmen de la Alcubilla del Caracol, but somewhat hidden down a cobblestone lane near the Alhambra Palace hotel, past the Fundación Rodríguez-Acosta. This is a lovely hillside villa with a large dining room, which boasts picture windows overlooking the city and a summer terrace affording spectacular and romantic views. Tel: 958 226 723.

Dining with a View of Alhambra
In the ancient Arab quarter of Albaicín

San Nicolás
Located at San Nicolás, 3, just west of the square of the same name, is one of several restaurants housed in romantic cármenes, with a lovely garden terrace for dining with spectacular frontal views of the Alhambra. Of all these restaurants-with-a-view, this one serves arguably the most memorable, truly gourmet cuisine, is the highest rated in the gourmet guides and has the most beautiful interior décor on two floors with stunning marble staircase. It opens for lunch at 1:00 and for dinner at 8:00. Closed Sunday night and Monday. Tel: 958 804 262.

Mirador de Morayma
Calle Pianista Garcia Carrillo, 2, just east of the Mirador of San Nicolás, this romantic spot, a former private mansion, serves an excellent tasting menu (degustación) for 30€. Clinton, Aznar and Kohl have all sampled its Arab-inspired delicacies. And the chef Mario Batali recently dined there while filming his PBS culinary road trip series, "Spain...On the Road Again", with Gwyneth Paltrow and Mark Bittman. Its wine list features Alpujarran (local) wines. The extremely pretty

gardens are an added plus. It opens for lunch at 1:30 and for dinner at 8:30. Tel: 958 228 290

El Huerto de Juan Ranas

Located just below the Mirador de San Nicolás at Callejón Atarazana Vieja, 8, this restaurant has a splendid vine covered outdoor terrace where both drinks and lunch are served plus a more formal, elegant and rather expensive restaurant downstairs, said to have been a favorite of King Fahd and the Saudi Royal Family. I would go here at sunset for a pre-dinner drink to soak up the sublime views of the "Red Fortress". Tel: 958 286 925.

Other options for dining with a view of the Alhambra in the upper Albaicín include **Carmen de la Verde Luna** at Camino Nuevo de San Nicolás, 16, **Las Tomasas** at Carril de San Agustín, 4, the **Mirador de Aixa**, next door at Carril San Agustín, 2, and **Carmen de Aben Humeya,** adjacent to the Cadima Wall (www.abenhumeya.com). But before booking, ask your hotel concierge, or desk staff, which of the above have had the best recent guest feedback. And remember that when dining at any of the above-mentioned spots in the Albaicín, you'll be shelling out more for the views than for the fine cuisine. Count on a minimum of 50€, or more, per person.

Dining Downtown

El Claustro

Located in the AC Palacio de Santa Paula Hotel, this is the most romantic and atmospheric setting for gourmet dining downtown, and my top choice for a special occasion (www.ac- hoteles.com). This dining venue is housed in the former cloister of the 1590 convent section of the beautiful hotel and has a stunning coffered wood ceiling and windows overlooking the courtyard. The avant-garde cuisine is a creation of chef Juan Andrés Rodríguez, who has won several prestigious gastronomic awards. Main courses are priced from 20€ - 26€ and all desserts priced at 7€. It opens for lunch at 1:30 and at 8:30 for dinner. Tel: 958 805 740.

Oliver

At Plaza Pescadería, 12, the restaurant is next door to the more famous, and somewhat more expensive, Cunini. On a recent visit, this friendly, welcoming, "we try harder" dining spot provided me my most memorable and relaxing downtown restaurant meal. You'll find a lively and attractive tapas bar in front, and an interior dining room divided into several cozy and pleasant alcoves with vaulted ceilings and pretty Andalusian décor. At my recent lunch it was packed to the rafters with hungry locals, not a tourist in sight, and service was prompt and polite (www.restauranteoliver.com). The menu focuses on seafood, as does Cunini's, but with gentler prices. My selection of *dorada* (porgy) proved delicious. Try their *tarta de yogur con frambuesas y trufas*, yoghurt cake with raspberries and chocolate truffles, for dessert. Oliver also serves typical Granadino dishes such as *habitas con jamón*, along with very fairly priced wines. Open Monday. Tel: 958 262 200.

Chikito

Plaza del Campillo, 9, has been a haunt of Granada's intellectual elite for years, the meeting place where García Lorca and friends held their tertulias (literary gatherings). Classic Granada dishes include braised oxtail stew, rabo de toro, and baby shrimp, quisquillas, straight from Motril on the coast. Chikito opens up an outdoor terrace on the square in summer and has a lively tapas bar. If you stick to the traditional dishes, you can have a very pleasant meal here at a reasonable cost. It opens for lunch at 1:00 and for dinner at 8:00. Closed Wednesday. Tel: 958 223 364.

Pilar del Toro

Located at Hospital de Santa Ana, 12, across the Carrera del Darro from the Plaza Nueva. This well regarded dining spot consists of an upstairs restaurant and downstairs bar set in the romantic courtyard of a 17th century home, a favorite local couples' watering hole. Tel: 958 225 470

Azafrán

Can be found at the beginning of the Paseo de los Tristes (at Paseo del Padre Manjón), the continuation of the Carrera del Darro, directly across from the river terraces, this casual-contemporary restaurant serves meals continuously, making it a handy stop for those who explore the Albaicín after a visit to the Alhambra. Try one of their varieties of couscous (lamb with raisins), their loin of pork with yoghurt and saffron sauce or one of their delicious salads. In the summer diners can eat al fresco on the wisteria-covered terrace across the street. Tel: 958 226 882

Puerta del Carmen

Located across from city hall, on the Plaza del Carmen downtown, this new tapas and small plates "hot spot" has a beautiful Belle Epoque décor, is both elegant and cozy and serves attractively presented plates of charcuterie, smoked fish, carpaccios, sushi-style and tostas or canapés.

The well-chosen wines are served in fine stemware, and everything here is presented in a sophisticated style (www.puertadelcarmenrestaurante.com). Call ahead for reservations: 958 223 737.

Dining in a Bullring

La Ermita

This is one of two dining venues located inside Granada's Plaza de Toros, dining below the seats of the bullring (www.grupoermita.com). La Ermita is the more formal, tablecloth dining of the two venues (dining room upstairs, tapas bar below) and specializes in grill meats - carnes al carbón. Phone: 958 290 257.

Tendido 1

The one next door serves tapas in a more informal setting of bullfight memorabilia and sherry casks. Opens daily from 11:00 am – 2:00 am (www.tendido1.com). You can have a full meal or just go for a bite, have a tapa or ración, such as a plate of

Trevélez ham, or cheese at the bar, or you can sit on the outdoor terrace in the summer. Phone: 958 272 302 / 958 278 769.

Tapas Bars Downtown

Tapas time in Granada begins before lunch, around 1:00 and before dinner, between 8:00 and 9:00.

Los Diamantes I & II
There are two tapas bars, the first on pedestrian Calle Navas, 26, and the newer cousin on Calle Rosario 12, a continuation of Navas, are the places to frequent for those who love pescaíto frito, battered and lightly fried fish tapas such as boquerones and anchovies, plus delicate batter fried eggplant, berenjena, all watered down by the local brew, an Alhambra beer. Both branches are closed on Sunday and Monday.

Bodegas Castañeda
On Calle Almireceros, 1, is a much-loved classic frequented by locals and students alike who flock here for the unpretentious fare and low prices. As in all the city bars, a free tapa is served along with your drink. Here I would stick to the tried and true-a plate of Trevélez ham and local cheese or one of their 18 varieties of stuffed potatoes.

Taberna Salinas
Also located on Calle Almireceros. Here you can enjoy a nice glass of wine and a montadito, an open-faced sandwich.

Bar Pasiegas
On Plaza de las Pasiegas opposite the cathedral is a designer, Basque-style pintxos bar.

Candela
On Calle Santa Escolastica, 9, the main drag that leads to the Realejo neighborhood, is a local's hangout for montaditos, a type of canapé with every type of topping imaginable.

La Taberna de Baco and La Opípara
Can be found on the south side of the Campo del Príncipe, the heart of the residential Realejo neighborhood. The best time to visit this "tapas bar central" is on a sultry summer night, when the terraces are open and packed with locals.

Tapas Bars in the ALBAICÍN

El Rincón del Aurora

Located on Plaza San Miguel Bajo, 7. This tiny bar with outdoor terrace has been recommended in Food and Wine (September '08) in an article regarding the filming of the PBS series, "Spain...On the Road Again". It was one the bars frequented by the series' protagonists, Chef Mario Batali and Mark Bittman during their filming.

Moroccan Style Tea Houses

Teterías

These funky, bohemian, pseudo-Moroccan tea lounges, opened by Moroccan immigrants, are quite in vogue these days among the university students or young at heart. Most are found in the area of the Albaicín now known as Little Morocco, on Calderería Nueva and Calderería Vieja, a souk-like bazaar filled with shops hawking wares imported from Morocco and other areas of the Middle East. These teahouses have an Arab atmosphere of dimly lit rooms, floors covered with carpets, horseshoe arches, marble columns and seating on velvet sofas piled with brightly colored cushions, with low carved wood tables, North African background music. All offer exotic teas - herbal, spice and fruit - plus shakes, batidos, sweet Arab pastries, such as baklava or khadaifi, and a drag on a narghile (hookah). Most are open from noon until midnight.

El Bañuelo Tetería

Bañuelo, 5,
near the Placeta de la Concepción.
It advertises itself as *"a little to drink, a little to eat and plenty of space"*.

Ice Cream

The city's best ice cream and horchata (a refreshing milk-like drink made of the Valencian chufa root) can be found at the super-popular

Los Italianos,

Gran Vía, 4.
Opens from March to October only.

Pastries

Regional pastry specialties, such as soplillos, cuajada de Carnaval and tortas mohínas can be found at Calle Reyes Católicos, 39, at the venerable **Pastelería López Mezquita**, a Granada tradition since 1862, open from 9:00 am until 11:00 pm.

Crepes

You'll find numerous bars with outdoor terraces on the Paseo de los Tristes, the continuation of the Carrera del Darro that runs along the river, directly across from the Alhambra hill, one of which, **Bar au lait**, specializes in crepes and coffees.

Churros and Chocolate

Grandadinos flock to the pretty Plaza Bib-Rambla downtown for their morning or late afternoon churros y chocolate treats at the **Gran Café Bib- Rambla** and the **Cafeteria Alhambra**.

Granada Shopping

Wandering the narrow walkways of the Alcaicería (behind the cathedral) and the streets of Calderería Nueva and Calderería Vieja in the lower Albaicín, referred to as "Little Morocco", you'll come across several souk-like markets filled with handicrafts, all imported from Morocco or the Middle East, which may or may not appeal. Nothing here is indigenous, but if you've never shopped in a medina, this is your chance to pick up some North African leather slippers. The Alcaicería stands at what was once the original Arab silk market, but is now a tourist - trinket - souvenir shop filled bazaar that for me at least, holds little appeal.

Handicrafts
Granada is known for two indigenous handicrafts: its pretty **Fajalauza** ware, the lovely pottery with blue and green designs on a white background, and an ancient craft known as **taracea** or marquetry. You'll find marquetry items galore in the shops on Cuesta Gomérez, the steep street leading up to the Alhambra and in the shops on the Alhambra hill as well. The craft consists of materials such as bone, metal, mother of pearl, inlaid in wood in intricate patterns. This craft dates from the 14th - 15th centuries. You'll find taracea jewelry boxes, picture frames, trays, mirrors, chess sets and backgammon boards, small tables and even writing desks.

Laguna Taracea
On the street leading from the Palace of Charles 5th, up to the Generalife gardens in the Alhambra complex, you'll pass the studios of Laguna Taracea where all the tour groups stop to see the artisans in action and purchase inexpensive gifts. When you enter the shop, head to the display room on your right and turn to the shelves on your right side for the genuine items inlaid with mahogany, rosewood, walnut and bone. The cheap, plastic touristy trinkets will be on your left.

Artesanía El Suspiro
The shop in town with the best, or widest selection of Granada's traditional blue, white and green Fajalauza pottery is Artesanía El Suspiro on the Plaza Santa Ana adjacent to the Plaza Nueva. The owners speak English.

Ceràmica Fabre
Plaza Pescadería 10

Guitars

Guitar aficionados will want to stop for a visit to Guitarrería Gil.
Guitarrería Gil
Plaza Realejo 15, 18009 Granada, Spain
+34 958 22 16 10

Wines

For a nice selection of wines, with 300 references from all the Spanish wine producing regions.
La Carte des Vins
Calle Navas, 29

Food
For gourmet food items, gastronomes must seek out the small but delightful

La Oliva,
Rosario, 9
The friendly, English speaking owner, Francisco Lillo, is a fountain of knowledge regarding Andalusian (and local) foods and wines and will help you with your selection of a perfect gift to take home.

Boutiques
Granada's most up-market shopping street is the boutique-lined **Angel Ganivet**, which runs southeast from the Puerta Real. Here you'll find a lovely children's clothing boutique, a Loewe luxury leather emporium and Salvador Bachiller designer shoes.

El Corte Inglés
Carrera del Genil, 20,
which has a very handy and vast basement supermarket for picnic items, snacks, wines and delicatessen products. The most selective gourmet items (such as the best of the Iberian *"bellota"* hams) are found in the "El Club de Gourmets" section. El Corte Inglés is open Monday - Saturday from 10:00 – 10:00. By law it can only open on eight Sundays during the year. To check the Sunday opening days in '08/09, see www.elcorteingles.es; at the bottom right of the home page under *centros comerciales*, click on *horarios y aperturas*, then *Andalucía*.

Walking Tours

Cicerone

Offers guided walking tours around the historical city center and the Albaicín that last approximately 2-1/2 hours (www.ciceronegranada.com). From March through October they depart from the meeting point, a kiosk at the Plaza Bib-Rambla at 10:30 am, and from November through February at 11 am. No reservations are needed; just arrive at the meeting point 10 - 15 minutes ahead of time. Cost: 12€. Children under 14 can come along for free. A 2€ voucher is available on line.

Full day Tours

Something out of the ordinary, especially for "foodies", is the new **Olive Oil Tour,** which is offered in English, French, or Spanish, and is a full-day tour to discover the varieties of olives, oils, to visit a traditional working mill and to experience new flavors.
The tour departs daily, picking participants up at their hotels between 9:30 – 10:00, returning between 3:30 – 4:00. The first stop is at a 15th century oil mill in Niguelas, where participants learn about the olive oil process and the different varieties and characteristics of olives, then it's on to an exhibition of more than 300 olive oils at a museum in Vélez de Benaudalla, followed by a tasting and time to purchase in the shop. The visit continues with a drive through the Lecrín Valley countryside and culminates with a paella lunch in a typical Andalusian mesón.
Book at www.oliveoiltour.com.

Entertainment

For relaxing, Arab sultan style, in a traditional Moorish bathhouse, a reproduction hammam, there are two bathhouses from which to choose:

Aljibe Baños Arabes
San Miguel Alta, 41, at the corner of Obispo Hurtado, is open daily, including holidays with passes at 10:00 am – 12:00 – 2:00 – 4:00 – 6:00 – 8:00 and 10:00 pm. Choose between a session in the hot and cold baths in 7 different pools of varying temperatures, or take the waters followed by a massage and aromatherapy. The bathhouse is only closed on Christmas Day. For a reservation call 958 522 867 (www.aljibesanmiguel.es)

Hammam
Calle Santa Ana, 16, off the Plaza Nueva, offers the same services as the above, but with an additional late night pass at 11:30.
Reserve online at: www.granada.hammamspain.com.

Flamenco
Although the city of Granada has produced some of the country's great flamenco artists, it can no longer be considered the premiere spot, outside of major festivals,

for experiencing the most genuine flamenco. The various tablaos or zambras in the caves of Sacromonte, from a flamenco purist point of view, simply don't put on a highly authentic or inspired show, full of duende (roughly defined as "soul") because they are geared solely to tourists. If you plan to travel on to Seville or Jerez, I suggest that you save your flamenco experience for those cities.

The only flamenco I recommend for authenticity would be the occasional Saturday night performances at the **Centro Internacional de Estudios Gitanos La Chumbera** on Camino del Monte in the Sacromonte neighborhood. Pick up a performance schedule at the tourist office.

A private, members-only flamenco club, or peña, **Peña Platería** is found deep in the heart of the Albaicín, at Placeta de Toqueros, 7, near San Miguel Bajo, opens its doors to non-members for its regular performances on Thursdays, and sometimes on Saturdays if visitors come in a small enough group. Performances begin at 10:30 pm. Inquire at the tourist office.
The **International Festival of Music and Dance** in late June-July includes on its yearly program the most important flamenco figures in Spain, such as Sara Baras, Antonio Canales, Eva Yerbabuena. And during the Festival de Otoño, the first week of December, the brightest stars of the flamenco world come to perform at the **Teatro Isabel la Católica,** Acera Del Casino.

Live music
Hidden away on Postigo de la Cuna, a little alleyway off Calle Azacayas (look for the name painted on the white wall), which is off the Gran Vía, you'll find a dark and smoky little bohemian bar and cavernous performing space, **El Eshavira**, where live jazz, world music and impromptu flamenco are performed on Thursdays and Sundays.
Also you can hear flamenco music at **Bar Soniquete** on the Carrera del Darro, 51, on Friday and Saturday at 11:00 pm. Cover charge: 10€, includes the first drink.

Dance clubs
A restored cinema is the venue for **Granada 10**, which plays movies and serves drinks during the evening and after midnight; it is transformed into a disco that hops until 6:00 am. Located just off the Gran Via at Calle Cárcel Baja, below Calle Elvira.

Accommodation Hotels

Parador San Francisco
Real de la Alhambra,
18009 Granada Granada
T: +34 958221440

Alhambra Palace
Plaza Arquitecto García de Paredes, 1,
18009 Granada, Spain
T: +34 958 22 14 68

Carmen de la Alcubilla del Caracol
Calle Aire Alta, 12,
18009 Granada, Spain
T: +34 958 21 55 51

Hotel América
Calle Real de la Alhambra, 53,
18009 Granada, Spain
T: +34 958 22 74 71

Hotel Guadalupe
Paseo de la Sabica,
18009 Granada, Spain
T: +34 958 22 57 30

Casa Morisca
Cuesta de la Victoria, 9,
18010 Granada, Spain
T: +34 958 22 11 00

Ladrón de Agua
Carrera del Darro, 13,
18010 Granada, Spain
T: +34 958 21 50 40

Casa del Capitel Nazarí
C/ Cuesta Aceituneros, 6, 18010
Granada, Spain
T: +34 958 21 52 60

AC Palacio de Santa Paula
Calle Gran Vía de Colón, 31,
18001 Granada, Spain
T: +34 958 80 57 40

Hospes Palacio de los Patos
Calle Solarillo de Gracia, 1,
18002 Granada, Spain
T: +34 958 53 57 90

Villa Oniria
Calle San Antón, 28,
18005 Granada, Spain
T: +34 958 53 53 58

Palacio de los Navas
Calle Navas, 1,
18009 Granada,
Spain +34 958 21 57 60

Hotel Reina Cristina
Calle Tablas, 4,
18002 Granada, Spain
T: +34 958 25 32 11

Hotel Anacapri
Calle Joaquín Costa, 7,
18010 Granada, Spain
T: +34 958 22 74 77

Macía Real de la Alhambra
Calle Mirador del Genil, 2,
18008 Granada, Spain
T: +34 958 21 66 93

Conversational Spanish Phrases

Greetings

Spanish-speaking countries are very polite societies and you must always be courteous and say "hello" and "how are you?". And don't worry about making mistakes.

Good morning – **Buenos días** (*bway nos dee ahs*)
Good afternoon – **Buenas tardes** (*bway nahs tar days*)
Good evening – **Buenas noches** (*bway nahs noh chayss*)
Hola (*oh lah*) is "hi" and you can say that with people you know.
¿Cómo está? (*coh moh es tah*) is "how are you?" if you don't know someone and ¿Cómo estás? (*coh moh es tahs*) if you do know them.

If they ask you how you are, you can say "good, thank you" – **"bien, gracias"** (*bee ayn, grah cee ahs*) because you, too, are a polite person.

Don't ever forget: Please – **Por favor** (*por fah vohr*) – and Thank you – **Gracias** (*grah cee ahs*). These are VERY IMPORTANT words in Spanish.

When you are introduced to someone, you say **"Mucho gusto"** (*moo choh goos toh*) and they will say the same thing back to you. It means, "nice to meet you."

¿Habla inglés? (*ahblah een glays*)? – Do you speak English? While it is never correct to *assume* that someone speaks English, you can ask if they do and they will like you so much better for asking in Spanish.

I want, I don't want – **Yo quiero, yo no quiero** (*yoh kee ayr oh, yoh noh kee ayr oh*)
I would like (more polite) – **Me gustaría** (*may goo stah ree ah*)
Where is – **¿Dónde está?** (*dohn des tah*)
How much does it cost – **¿Cuánto cuesta?** (*cwahn toh cways tah*)?
What time is it? – **¿Qué hora es?** (*kay orah ess*)?
Do you have? – **¿Tiene?** (*tee ayn ay*)?
I have, I don't have – **Yo tengo, yo no tengo** (*yoh tayn goh, yoh noh tayn goh*)
I understand, I don't understand – **Yo entiendo, yo no entiendo** (*yoh ayn tee ayn doh, yoh noh ayn tee ayn doh*)
Do you understand? – **¿Entiende?** (*ayn tee ayn day*)?
I want a ticket, a hotel, a taxi – **Yo quiero un boleto, un hotel, un taxi** (*yoh kee ayr oh oon boh lay toh, oon oh tayl, oon tahk see*)
Where is a restaurant? – **¿Dónde está un restaurante?** (*dohn days tah oon rays tore rahn tay*)?
A train? – **¿Un tren?** (*oon trayn*)?
The street ... ? – **¿La calle ... ?** (*lah cah yay*)?
A bank? – **¿Un banco?** (*oon bahn coh*)?
Where is the bathroom? – **¿Dónde está el baño?** – (*dohn days tah ayl ban yoh*)?

I want a hotel, I want a hotel with a bathroom – **Yo quiero un hotel, yo quiero un hotel con baño** (*yoh kee ayr oh oon oh tel, yo kee ayr oh oon ohtel cohn bahn yoh*)
I need – **Yo necesito** (*yoh nay say see toh*). Very useful, and you can supply the noun.
Yo necesito un hotel, un cuarto, un cuarto con baño – (*yoh nay say see toh oon oh tayl, oon cwar toh, oon cwar toh cohn ban yoh*)
Where is the exchange? ; Where is a bank? – **¿Dónde está una casa de cambio?** (*dohn days tah oon ah cah sah day cahm bee oh*) ;
¿Dónde está el banco? (*dohn days tah ayl bahn coh*)?
Money – **Dinero** (*dee nayr oh*).

Once you have asked a question, someone will answer you in Spanish. Here are some simple directions that someone may give you, to turn right, to turn left, or to go straight ahead. Listen for these key words:

Right – **A la derecha** (*a lah day ray chah*)
Left – **A la izquierda** (*ah lah eez kee ayr dah*)
Straight ahead – **Derecho** (*Day ray choh*)
At the corner – **En la esquina** (*a lah ays kee nah*)
In one, two, three, four blocks – **A una cuadra, a dos, tres, cuatro cuadras** – (*a oona dohss, trayss, cwah troh cwah drahs*)
Dining Out: What do you want to eat or drink?
Probably the most useful phrases you will need are in a restaurant. Ask for anything by using "quiero" (kee ayr oh) or "quisiera" (kee see ayr oh) – "I want" or "I would like." And remember to say "por favor" and "gracias"!
A table – **Una mesa** (*oona may sah*)
A table for two, three, four – **Una mesa para dos tres, cuatro** (*oona may sah pah rah dohss, trays, kwah troh*)
A menu – **Un menú** (*oon may noo*)
Soup – **Sopa** (*soh pah*)
Salad – **Ensalada** (*ayn sah lah dah*)
Hamburger (Another necessity!) – **Hamburguesa** (*ahm boor gay sah*)
With ketchup, mustard, tomato, lettuce – **Con salsa de tomate, mostaza, tomate, lechuga** – (*cohn sahl sah day toh mah tay, mohs tah sah, toh mah tay, lay choo gah*)
An appetizer – **Una entrada** (*oona ayn trah dah*)
Dessert – **Un postre** (*oon pohs tray*)
A drink – **Una bebida** (*oona bay bee dah*)
Water – **Agua** (*ah gwah*)
Red wine, white whine – **Vino tinto** (*vee noh teen toh*), **vino blanco** (*vee noh blahn coh*)
Beer – **Cerveza** (*sayr vay sah*)
Coffee – **Un café** (*oon cah fay*)
Calling a waiter or waitress – **¡Señor! or ¡Señorita!** (*say nyor, say nyor eetah*)
The check – **La cuenta** (*lah cwayn tah*)

More Information

Credit cards. Many places in smaller towns still do not take credit cards so make sure you have enough cash with you. You can ask if you can use a credit card – **una tarjeta de credito** (oonah tar hey tah day cray dee toh).

If you have questions, you can always use a noun with a question.

For example, you can pull out your credit card and say: **¿Tarjeta de credito?** They will understand.

An all-purpose word: **No funciona** (*noh foonk see oh nah*) – It doesn't work! You can use this for a million circumstances! Just point at the shower or whatever and say "¡No funciona!"

Lastly don't be afraid to make mistakes, have fun with the language, nobody learned a new language without making mistakes, and does that say they can't learn a new language are usually the same ones that say they are afraid to make mistakes.

Made in the USA
Columbia, SC
27 September 2023

23461519R00076